ISBN: 9798863784373

Acknowledgements: The author would especially like to thank Paul Jossart and Steve Price for reviewing the 1st draft of this book and Tim Coughlin and Tim Deckers for reviewing the 2nd draft, correcting mistakes, and suggesting improvements. The author is eternally grateful to Hutchinson Technology, Inc. for providing extensive training in Quality methods and tools, for providing the opportunity to use these tools on problems at work, and for their generous tuition reimbursement program. The author would also like to thank his family and friends for their patience while he was doing schoolwork at all hours of the day, during vacations, school activities, etc. Wife Kari and children Kraig and Katy showed particular patience and support in this regard.

Foreword:

With more than 40 years' experience in manufacturing, design, and R&D in the disk drive, medical device, ag equipment, and machining industries, I have dealt with hundreds of companies including employers, suppliers, customers, and students in my various roles. The quality myths and lessons learned discussed in this book have either come up repeatedly during my career or have caused such confusion/consternation when they did arise as to make a lasting impact with a single occurrence. Some time ago I became frustrated with repeatedly solving the same problems and decided there has to be a way to "get the message out" faster than one company and one person at a time. That eventually led me to start a consulting business and create this book.

The book is a compilation of many topics arranged in individual chapters, the common thread being that the topics all relate to quality or reliability of products, processes, or service. The first edition focused entirely on topics that have proven to be problematic for many people across multiple companies. This second edition is expanded to include topics that have proven beneficial, and/or are unique even if not particularly problematic, as well as some anecdotes.

Some of the subjects in this book will speak equally well to people just entering the workforce in entry level jobs, to senior management and those in between. Others require a level of background knowledge and skills that may not be in the current repertoire of all readers, particularly the latter chapters which are more mathematical in nature. The book is broken into two primary focus areas: how to effectively view Quality Management principles and apply them in your daily work and a more technical approach to practical application of statistical methods. The intention of this book is not to teach the fundamental statistical methods behind the latter subjects, rather to help people become more effective by providing specific recommendations and provoking curiosity and encouraging further study.

The back of the book includes a short synopsis of the chapters. This synopsis will:
- Provide a reference to help readers quickly find information.
- Identify the intended audience for individual chapters.
- List any background knowledge necessary for readers to obtain maximum benefit from the information.

For the statistical methods discussed, I am a firm believer that true understanding of an engineering or statistical technique requires an understanding of the science and math underlying the technique. If the subject of a chapter sparks your interest, but you don't as of today have the background to grasp it fully, I would strongly encourage you to pursue that knowledge. There are many excellent resources available for this type of training and/or education, some of which are listed at the back of the book, along with a short explanation of selected references.

I hope you find the subjects and advice useful in your job. The overall goal is to ethically improve business performance and help people become more effective in whatever career they choose. The book has a strong Manufacturing emphasis, reflecting my experience. However, many of the concepts can easily be extended to other industries. Examples:
- "These parts need to ship today. . ." can easily translate into the service industry if the wording changes to "I need to make X number of phone calls today", "I need to get Y customers through per hour", etc.
- "If Management Rewards Firefighting. . ." concepts can apply anywhere.
- Normalization of Deviance (see chapter 2 for more explanation) can arise in any organization.
- "We know we've shipped this before. . ." is analogous with "Our service might not be the best, but people keep coming back."
- Principle-based business concepts are universal.
- Etc., etc., etc.

I hope you find the information here useful and thought-provoking.

3

2nd Edition enhancements include:

- Multiple new chapters, including what's likely to be the most controversial chapter – Set Your Own Course (To Thine Own Self Be True - William Shakespeare)
- Additional mathematical treatment of topics from sampling to reliability
  - Designing Time Accelerated Tests
  - Effect of Measurement Error on Process Capability
  - Derivation of Attribute Sample Size Rule of Thumb
- The Great Unsolved Quality Problem of Our Time
- Short Bites – topics that didn't seem to warrant a chapter unto themselves
  - Thermodynamics (entropy) in the workplace
  - Million-dollar question
  - Most difficult decision
  - Rigid rules loosely enforced or loose rules rigidly enforced?
- Changed from color to black and white. While this is not a content enhancement, color proves to be too expensive with print on demand, making the price higher than seems proper.

Best of luck in all your endeavors.
Kevin

Contents

Acronyms and Definitions

21CFR820: Code of Federal Regulations Title 21 Part 820 – Quality System Regulation. Also referred to as GMP (Good Manufacturing Practices) or cGMP (current Good Manufacturing Practices).

ANSI: American National Standards Institute

ANSI Z1.4: Sampling Procedures and Tables for Inspection by Attributes. This industry standard lists sampling plans for attribute acceptance sampling

AOQ: Average Outgoing Quality. AOQ represents the quality level (i.e. percentage of nonconforming units) expected to be shipped to the customer given a stated acceptance sampling level and incoming quality level. Perfect inspection is often assumed in the analysis even though inspection is typically less than perfect.

AOQL: Average Outgoing Quality Limit. The worst case for AOQ across the range of possible quality values coming to acceptance sampling.

AQL: Acceptance Quality Level. ANSI Z1.4 defines AQL as "The AQL is the quality level that is the worst tolerable process average when a continuing series of lots is submitted for acceptance sampling."

ASQ: American Society for Quality

BOK: Body Of Knowledge. This text uses the acronym to refer to the relevant ASQ BOK for a given profession. ASQ describes the BOK as ". . . the scope and extent of the knowledge that would be expected of any professional within that field.".

CAPA: Corrective Action / Preventive Action

Check-the-box exercise: When someone performs a task in a sloppy manner, without proper diligence, just to say it was completed.

Cpk: A particular form of process capability index. Cpk can be used to estimate the proportion of nonconforming product produced by a given process under controlled conditions. See chapter 28 for formulae and further explanation.

DHR: Device History Record. This is defined in 21CFR820 as "a compilation of records containing the production history of a finished device".

DOE: (statistical) Design Of Experiments. A technique to improve efficiency and save money by concurrently testing the effect of multiple parameters.

FDA: United States Food and Drug Administration

FMEA: Failure Modes and Effects Analysis. An engineering method used to predict, and then prevent, problems. Sometimes referred to as FMECA – Failure Modes, Effects, and Criticality Analysis.

FTA: Fault Tree Analysis.

ISO: International Organization for Standardization

ISO 13485: The international standard used for the development and monitoring of Quality Management Systems in the medical device industry. Title of the standard is "Medical devices – Quality management systems – Requirements for regulatory purposes". The requirements in this standard are similar to those in 21CFR820.

LCL: Lower Control Limit

LSL: Lower Specification Limit

LTPD: Lot Tolerance Percent Defective is that quality level that we wish to have a high confidence of rejecting when performing acceptance sampling.

MDR: Medical Device Regulation 21017/745. This directive outlines the requirements to apply the CE mark and sell medical devices in Europe.

MTBF: Mean Time Between Failures. The mean (average) times between failures in a repairable device. Implies constant failure rate and is frequently misused.

MTTF: Mean Time To Failure. The mean (average) time to failure.

MTTFF: Mean Time To First Failure. The mean (average) time to the first failure of a device than can fail more than once.

NCR: NonConforming (or NonConformance) Report

Normalization of Deviance: When behaviors slowly change over time resulting in the acceptance of inappropriate behavior

Pareto: A bar chart used to prioritize activities by illustrating which problems, causes of problems, etc. occur most frequently.

Pencil whipping: Approving a document without proper/adequate review. Sometimes also used to refer to someone writing down a value different than the measured value to make a nonconforming product appear conforming.

Ppk: A particular form of process capability index. Ppk can be used to estimate the proportion of nonconforming product produced by a given process under controlled conditions. See chapter 28 for formulae and further explanation.

Process validation: Establishing by objective evidence that a process consistently produces a result or product meeting its predetermined specifications. (FDA, 21CFR 820)

QA: Quality Assurance

QC: Quality Control

QE: Quality Engineering or Quality Engineer

QI: Quality Inspector

QMS: Quality Management System

r^2: The coefficient of determination in regression analysis. The proportion of variation in the dependent variable that is explained by the stated mathematical (regression) model.

R&D: Research and Development

RDD: Rigid Disk Drive (in a computer)

RE: Reliability Engineer

ROI: Return On Investment

Root Cause Analysis (RCA): A systematic investigative method to determine the most basic cause of a failure. The investigation often will stop at a cause that can be controlled by the organization and, when controlled, will prevent the failure from recurring even if this is not the most basic (true root) cause.

SOP: Standard Operating Procedure

SPC: Statistical Process Control

10

UCL: Upper Control Limit

USL: Upper Specification Limit

WI: Work Instruction

1 These Parts Need to Ship Today

Rarely have 6 words created more consternation in the world of Quality. Pressure to accept product before the last truck of the day leaves is a common situation throughout industry and, if improperly handled, can result in negative consequences such as:

- Shipment of nonconforming product due to time pressure **causing mistakes** in Quality.
- Shipment of nonconforming product due to **pressure to ship under any circumstance**.
- Taking shortcuts, resulting in acceptance of nonconforming product.
- Upset customers and potentially lost business resulting from the aforementioned nonconforming product.
- Potential liability for the company, depending on contracts and whether the nonconforming product can lead to harm.
- Tension between the Quality department and other departments.
- An "us vs. them" mentality within the Quality department.
- High stress-related turnover in Quality. It's difficult to have pride in workmanship if one feels constantly under pressure to either take shortcuts or accept nonconforming product.
- High cost and reduced efficiency, both from a culture that fosters an adversarial relationship between Quality and other departments and from the inevitable returns/scrap when shortcuts are taken.
- Etc.

So, how should these words (these parts need to ship today) be interpreted? We all want our companies to succeed and this can only happen if we satisfy our customers. The problems arise when we sacrifice the long term for the short term by accepting nonconforming product, either intentionally or unintentionally due to time pressure.

Shipping nonconforming product is much worse than delaying a shipment by a day. If the customer cannot use the product, we have in effect delayed the shipment by the length of time required for shipping (2x – there and

12

back), customer incoming inspection and MRB (Material Review Board), and the time required for us to sort or re-manufacture the nonconforming product. If the product makes it into the customer's lines or worse yet into the field, the costs multiply – sometimes by more than 100x.

Here's how the Quality department should react to the statement "these parts need to ship today":
- Do our best to complete tasks as quickly as possible – under the constraint that those tasks are performed correctly
- No shortcuts
- Only proper practices
- Communicate the status of the product in the best and quickest manner possible
- If conforming, complete paperwork and contact shipping to notify that the product is ready to ship
- If nonconforming, create NCR (NonConformance Report) as expeditiously as possible and let the proper people know that the NCR exists so that it can be dealt with appropriately
- Re-audit in a timely manner
- Ask for help if necessary

The Quality department is always on the end of the whip in the sense that it is the last step before shipping and, if the shipment is already late, the expectation can **appear** as though Quality is being asked to complete their task in an impossibly short time. It may be that on occasion Quality is given parts ½ hour before the last shipment and there is no way to legitimately complete the audit in less than 2 hours, even with extra help. In that situation, forcing completion in time to meet the scheduled shipment would place the customer, and the company's reputation, at risk.

Management creates the culture in a company through policies, words, and **actions**. Quality Inspectors/Auditors will modify their own actions to fit within this culture. It is therefore incumbent upon management to create and promote the desired culture. If management promotes shortcuts, Quality will follow that lead. Management that holds firm to the idea that

13

the first principle is "do it right" and the second principle is "do it quickly" subject to the first principle, creates a true culture for success. This is one instance where "appearance is reality". That is, if Quality feels that management is pressing to get the product shipped, they will react accordingly even if management's true intention is to ensure everything is correct prior to shipping.

In my experience, people in the Quality department often are prone to interpret unclear or ambiguous direction from management in a manner that encourages shortcuts. I've been in many situations where upper management is promoting the proper culture, but somehow the message gets changed or misunderstood between upper management and Manufacturing/Quality personnel. Promoting proper culture requires constant reinforcement.

2 Principle-Based Business

Stephen Covey in <u>The 7 Habits of Highly Effective People</u> wrote about the benefits of a principle-based life. The same concept applies to a business. Many times, people in different departments will be working at cross-purposes in a business. Example: the Manufacturing department may view its job as "getting the product past Quality" while the Quality department views its job as "catching the stuff that Manufacturing is trying to sneak past us". This leads to:

- Inefficiencies
- Disagreements
- Inconsistent image presented to customers
- Inconsistent information given to customers
- Reduced customer trust in the company
- Higher cost
- Lower profit
- Confusion
- Lower employee morale

A sample set of principles could be along the lines of:

Principle 1: Our company will always maintain compliance with regulations and industry standards
   a) 21CFR 820, ISO 13485, and MDR take precedence over internal procedures.
   b) Lack of a company procedure is not justification for failure to comply with regulations or industry standards.
   c) In case of a conflict between internal procedures and regulations/industry standards, our company will follow 21CFR 820, ISO 13485, and MDR.

Principle 2: Our company will comply with all aspects of customer agreements.

15

Principle 3: Subject to principles 1 and 2, our employees will follow internal procedures, even if we believe a better way may exist. When we believe a better way exists, the proper course of action is to submit a change request to update the procedure. A deviation often suffices for a temporary solution while the formal change request is being processed, under the assumption that the deviation undergoes proper review and approval.

Principle 4: Within the constraints of the above principles, we will strive to perform our duties in the most efficient manner possible.
   a) The most stringent or conservative possible interpretation of an industry standard is not necessarily the right one. It can be very difficult to author a document in a manner that can only be interpreted one way and industry standards and regulations need to apply to a broad range of businesses – interpretation is typically required. The most conservative possible interpretation of a given set of words may be completely contrary to the intent of the author/approvers.
      1) Example: I've worked in companies where the standard was interpreted such that every department was required to approve every document that might be related. This has led to 10 or more required signatures where only 2 were really necessary.
      2) Example: CFR 820 gives companies the option of using a paper-based or electronic system for storing quality records. If a company chooses electronic, the requirements of part 11 apply. Multiple software solutions are available that will comply with part 11 and, within a software package, decisions must be made regarding configuration. The optimal configuration for a large company may not be the same as the optimal configuration for a small one.
      3) Many different versions of procedures may comply with principle 1. In such a case, we should choose the one that is both compliant and most efficient to maximize customer and employee satisfaction and profits.

As implied, earlier principles supersede later principles. For example, no argument for efficiency may be used to justify a practice that fails to comply with industry standards. Likewise, the presence of an internal procedure does not justify a practice that fails to comply with regulations.

Being able to point to a set of guiding principles, known by all employees, leads to:
- Better compliance with regulations and industry standards
- Quicker and better decisions
- More consistent decisions across departments
- Decisions that conform to expectations of senior management
- Improved customer satisfaction
- Improved employee satisfaction
- Improved efficiency
  o Lower cost
  o Higher profit

These high-level guiding principles lead to development of lower level principles that may even more directly aid in specific decision-making.

Example 2.1: an inspection sheet is messy and the customer has requested we don't send it in that state. The person who created the original is not in the office. The parts need to ship. Is it ok for someone else to re-copy the inspection sheet and either sign their name or sign the original inspector's name? Rather lengthy discussions can ensue (and have ensued) around questions such as this. If we revert to principle-based business, the answer is rather obvious.
- In addition to the above principles, we should add that a DHR (Device History Record) needs to "tell the story" of how the parts were built by accurately recording all of the important information.
- Signing your name when you did not perform the inspection does not comply because it implies the inspection was done by someone other than the person who did it and constitutes falsification of data.
- Signing the other person's name doesn't comply as this would constitute forgery.

- Sending the messy inspection sheet does not comply with management or customer wishes.
- How do we comply with the stated principles and management's wishes? Re-copy the measurement sheet, keep the original with the DHR, and add a statement to the re-copied sheet along the lines of "Measurement sheet re-copied for clarity. Original retained with DHR." The person creating the re-copied sheet will sign and date this statement. We might choose to place a similar statement on the original to indicate the existence of a re-copied version.

Example 2.2: Customer notification of a problem. Running a principle-based business can change the question from "Should we tell the customer?" to "What is the best way to tell the customer?". These two questions are very different from one another. Note: customer may be a corporate customer or FDA/end use customer in case of a recall. In certain circumstances involving principles 1 and/or 2, the answer to the first question is pre-ordained – the customer needs to be informed - and having that discussion will take up valuable time that would be better spent answering the second question. Considerations related to the second question include:

- Are we certain of the conclusion? Providing misleading information resulting from a lack of due diligence is not in the best interest of the company or the customer.
    - Have the correct data been collected?
    - Has the analysis been verified?
    - Are different conclusions as plausible as the original one that led to the need to inform the customer?
    - Have we taken the proper steps since becoming aware of the situation?
    - Is there any other information of which the customer needs/wants to be aware?
    - Are all actions happening in a timely manner?
- Who is creating the customer communication?

- It's very possible to present the same facts using different approaches/methods that will result in different reactions from a given audience.
- Facts should be presented as unambiguously as possible without either minimizing or exaggerating the implications.
- The original communication should make clear to the customer what actions have been/are being taken to address the situation.

- Of course, the business world isn't always straightforward and the first question is often very relevant. A principle-based business makes both the decisions easier – whether the customer needs to be notified as well as how to communicate once the need has been identified. Without guiding principles, companies can get caught up in whether or not to notify the customer for inordinate amounts of time.

Example 2.3: Employee safety is a key principle. I was the Management Safety representative at a company. A night crew lead came to me with a concern about a new procedure. The procedure had the employees placing gloved, protected hands into a bath with dangerous chemicals. The protection was adequate when intact, but the employees were uncomfortable. What if the glove developed a leak or some of the solution was splashed? A principle-based decision was easy. Even though the procedure was safe with proper precautions, the potential hazard was unnecessary. As management rep, I refused to approve the procedure even though it meant the job would not be completed on time. Net result? The engineers quickly devised a safer and better alternative for use on this and all future jobs.

Example 2.4: A Document Control department desires to minimize the number of controlled Work Instructions in Manufacturing due to the time required to maintain multiple copies and the increased risk for mistakes, such as obsolete revisions remaining in Manufacturing, inherent in the maintenance of a larger number of copies. The number of controlled Work Instructions needs to be adequate for Manufacturing personnel to have easy access to them, otherwise how can we possibly ensure we are

19

complying with principle 1 and following the Work Instructions in an efficient manner? Yes, this is more work and time for the Document Control department but the added time in Document Control is more than offset by the added procedural compliance and improved efficiency in Manufacturing. This example illustrates another lower level principle that follows directly from main principles – company-wide considerations override department or personal considerations. Principle 4 (efficiency) needs to be considered from the largest perspective first (company rather than department).

Many of you are reading this thinking "of course we run a principle-based business". You are probably right. Remember that it's not enough to have these principles understood and followed by senior management, rather they must be communicated and promoted throughout the organization to have maximum effectiveness. Anything worthwhile requires effort to maintain and improve. You might want to ask yourself:

- Are the principles clearly articulated and communicated?
- Do all employees understand the principles and if they are consistently enforced throughout the various levels of management?
- How did you determine the answer to the previous questions?
- Do you have objective evidence to demonstrate whether the principles are being consistently applied?
- How often are the principles reinforced in communications with all levels of employees?

Answering yes to these questions will help ensure the business is being run in a consistent, efficient manner that will foster success.

A principle-based approach to business is one of the best ways to avoid a particularly insidious problem known as Normalization of Deviance. Normalization of Deviance is when behaviors slowly change over time resulting in the acceptance of inappropriate behavior. Since it occurs slowly over time, individuals and companies don't often realize this is happening. I first learned this concept from a Minneapolis Star/Tribune article. Someone who had worked in the financial industry had just gotten out of jail. He described a highly competitive culture at his former employer wherein employees were competing for the largest bonus. The internal competition was so fierce that to receive maximum bonus, employees had to push the rules. Before long everyone was doing so and to receive maximum bonus, employees needed to break the rules and push the bounds of ethics. This slowly migrated to unethical and eventually illegal behavior. He got caught, went to jail, and told the story to the newspaper after he was released. It was easy to see how this type of situation could arise at any company. It's insidious because it's a slow migration in the values or operating procedures of a business, spanning months or years. Each step on the journey may be a small step that makes sense from the starting point of the preceding step. This "journey" is illustrated graphically below.

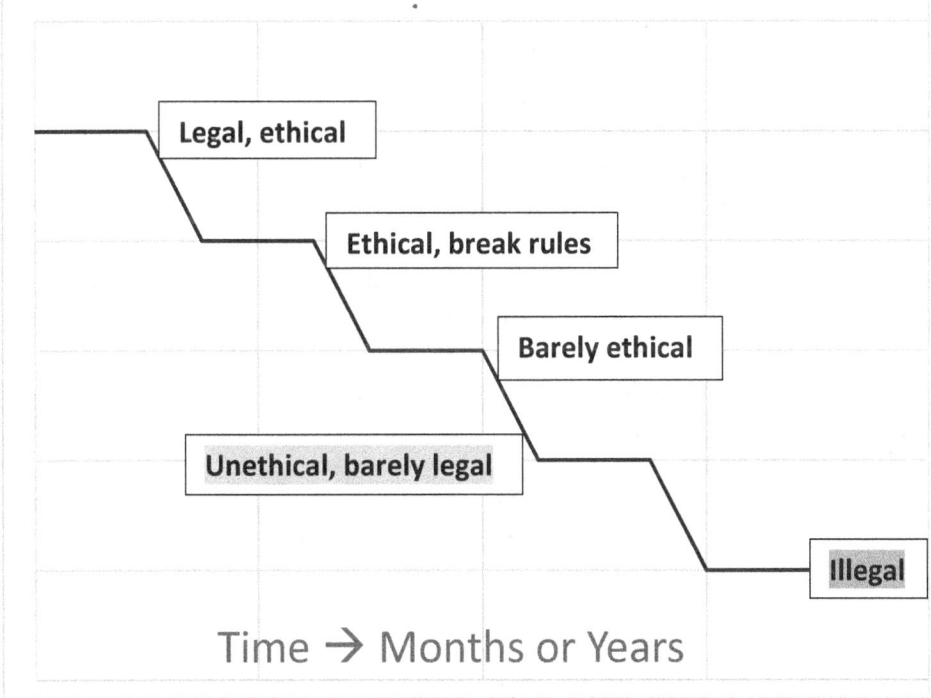

Figure 2.1 – Normalization of Deviance

A principle-based business, where the principles are well communicated, has hundreds or thousands of opportunities for employees to recognize this

21

type of change in behavior before it becomes unethical or illegal. Examples of normalization of deviance are easy to find. A few are detailed below, along with the source when available. All examples other than the above referenced story were found on the internet and certain pages were no longer available at the time this was written.

- Space shuttle Columbia – foam had broken off on previous shuttle flights. This caused much concern the first few times but became accepted as normal after multiple occurrences until the day it brought down the shuttle. Sources: 1. Transcript (Part 5): Hearing on the Space Shuttle Columbia Investigation Before the Senate Committee on Commerce, Science & Transportation 14 May 2003. 2. http://www.westgard.com/guest25.htm
- Fire prevention practices degraded until an explosion killed 1 and injured 6. Source: REPORT NO. 2004-01-I-IN SEPTEMBER 2005, U.S. Chemical Safety and Hazard Investigation Board.
- Miniscribe, a disk drive company had a culture with very high pressure to meet financial objectives. This eventually led to:
  - o Shipping bricks as completed disk drives
  - o Falsifying inventory and accounting figures
  - o Shipping obsolete and scrap products as good product
  - o It's unfathomable that someone woke up one morning and decided to do this. It's much more believable that this culture slowly developed over a period of time

Source: http://articles.latimes.com/1989-09-13/business/fi-2051_1_massive-fraud

- In 2016, Wells Fargo was caught opening accounts for customers without customer knowledge or approval. This resulted from a culture with aggressive sales targets and inadequate emphasis on principles/ethics. Source: https://www.wellsfargo.com/about/press/2017/independent-investigation-findings_0410/
- In 2016, VW paid $15B to settle a case related to use of software to cheat on emissions tests. **Opinion:** It's difficult to believe someone woke up one day and said "hey, I wonder if we can get

away with this". It's much more believable that the cheating was a result of many small steps starting with something more innocent, along the lines of "let's make sure we don't ever have a false failure of emissions tests".

How else can this happen in industry?

- A process change that is marginal, but should result in customer notification is approved without notification. This "marginal" situation becomes a "no notification required" situation and slightly more significant changes are now viewed as marginal. Over time, the need for customer notification/approval can be rationalized away even for quite significant changes that clearly require approval prior to implementation.
- Horseplay/unsafe practices can become accepted over time.
- Product or process validation practices may slowly change to the point they are insufficient.
- Approving change orders without proper justification can result in a continual degradation in the amount of effort put into those justifications.
- Approving marginal corrective actions to customer complaints or CAPAs can result in a lower standard for future corrective actions and a continuing downward spiral in those standards.
- Approving marginal engineering reports can result in a downward spiral in the usefulness of future reports.
- Allowing poor service might not result in immediate complaints, but over time the level of service degrades to the point that most customers no longer return.

Example 2.5: A colleague conveyed to me the following story. I did not observe any of it first-hand, but have reason to believe it's factual as remembered by that colleague. It's important to point out this product was very easily damaged as that is the apparent initiator for the normalization of deviance.

1. QC started out by taking their own measurements.
2. QC had less experience than Mfg handling the product, so QC started to ask the Mfg operator to measure their sample while QC

watched and recorded the data. Unethical or illegal? No, the intentions were good and the integrity of the measurements was maintained.

3. After a period of time, and since they were busy, QC asked the Mfg operators to record the measurements for them and they (QC) would then sign the form as if they had taken the measurements themselves. We now have a problem since the QC personnel who signed the inspection form weren't present when the measurements were taken and didn't record any of the data themselves.

4. The Mfg operators would generally measure the QC sample immediately after their in-process measurements. The measurements on consecutive parts, as might be expected, were very close so eventually the Mfg operators stopped measuring the QC parts and just wrote down the same result measured on the in-process sample – or, if they were astute about being caught fabricating data, wrote down very similar measurements for the QC data. We have two problems here, one with statistics and the other with ethics/legality.

   o First, the sampling problem. The QC sample is not intended to be the same as the Manufacturing sample, yet measuring consecutive parts for in-process and QC samples had the net result of making the samples virtually identical.

   o Second, recording "measurements" that weren't actually taken represents falsification of data which is a serious breach of ethics and, in regulated industries, illegal.

This is a good example of normalization of deviance. The change from step 1 to step 2 by itself does not seem very large and is not a particular reason for concern. An operator who started after step 2 became the norm would not know any different and moving to step 3 might not seem like a big change. One could understand how an operator who started after step 3 became the norm might think "this is a waste of time to measure twice as many parts when the numbers are always basically identical anyway". Operators don't often receive much training regarding the topic of data integrity. While it seems obvious to many of us that fabricating measurements is wrong, I've unfortunately seen that exact practice multiple times throughout my career.

To summarize, making decisions based on a fixed set of principles will improve the efficiency, consistency, and quality of those decisions as well as help avoid the insidious problem of normalization of deviance.

3 "In God we trust, all others bring data." Author Unknown

Have you ever taken action on something you've been told only to find out later that the information was not accurate or not complete? Was this embarrassing? Did you feel foolish? I have. It's not a good feeling and immediately reminded me that a more deliberative approach usually results in better decisions.

Have you made decisions without bothering to collect information only to find out later that the decision was wrong and not supported by data? Did this result in unnecessary expense? Again, I have unfortunately done this, but fortunately learned from it.

Too often in business, decisions are made based on opinion; often the person with the most charisma, loudest voice, most tenacious argument, etc. will have the most impact on a decision. These decisions often benefit the influential person at the expense of the business.

Example 3.1: someone comes into your office and tells you they are finding mistakes on our prints (engineering drawings) and it is a problem that needs to be fixed right away. This example happened to me almost verbatim.

- What are the problems? Are they simple typos where the meaning is obvious or dimensioning errors that would lead to non-functioning or potentially even hazardous product?
- How frequent are the problems? Are they on 1% of the prints, 10% of the prints, was it an isolated incident?
- Are there patterns to the problems? Do they primarily occur on prints from a single product family? Assembly vs. component prints? A certain department within the company? Other?

The person could not answer any of the above questions and expected me to act on faith and take immediate action. I refused to do so since all this data could be found with little effort and it seems self-evident how one could waste time and effort trying to fix the wrong problem if the data

26

were not gathered prior to taking action. It turns out the issues "weren't large enough to warrant the minimal effort required to find the data" and thus weren't large enough to warrant immediate action. Of course we want 100% accurate drawings. Understanding this, drawing errors can have very different consequences depending on the type of error. Identification of a single error does not a crisis make.

Example 3.2: An NCR is written stating that parts were manufactured out of customer tolerance and it is unknown when the problem started. Should we notify the customer? A simple analysis of all of the data indicates that the o.o.t. (out of tolerance) part is a clear outlier compared to the rest of the data. Furthermore, the outlier appears to be an incorrect data entry. While it might require additional data collection, it can be demonstrated with high confidence that this data point is a simple typo. Alternatively, investigation might conclude that the part in question was measured incorrectly. In either case, concluding that nonconforming product was produced and possibly shipped would be incorrect. Rather than serving the customer, drawing the incorrect conclusion simply creates confusion and unnecessary work for everyone, customer included. Data is required for the correct conclusion to be reached.

Example 3.3: A customer complains about poor service so the employee is reprimanded or maybe even fired. Investigation/data would have shown that the employee behaved correctly throughout the encounter and this customer was in fact belligerent toward that particular employee due to preconceived notions (prejudice) on the part of the customer and based on employee's ethnicity or lifestyle.

Example 3.4: Passrate at QC final audit from a particular manufacturing line is 100% and that line is due to be rewarded based on this. QC passrate is data, so all is good, right? What if investigation/further data collection shows a low passrate at the customer for product from this particular line? This might imply that the QC passrate data is faulty and not to be believed. Hypothetical? Hardly. Rather, I have observed this multiple times throughout my career. QC Inspectors are susceptible to pressure from people in Manufacturing and can be coerced into accepting product that should be rejected. Even though one can argue that rewarding the line is a data-based decision (based on QC passrate), the data is faulty. This leads to a corollary: In God we trust, all others bring data – and be ready to prove the data are valid.

Example 3.5: A grit blasting process was used at a supplier. It was "general knowledge" that the grit blast process changes part dimensions and we should manufacture the part larger before grit blast to meet nominal after grit blast. This was supported by scientific reasoning – grit blasting can remove material. The data, when analyzed, failed to show the expected relationship. It turns out the specific process was not very aggressive and, combined with the part hardness, resulted in no noticeable change in dimensions.

Dr. Deming also said on page 121 of <u>Out of the Crisis</u> "the most important figures that one needs for management are unknown or unknowable (Lloyd S. Nelson, director of statistical methods for the Nashua corporation), but successful management must nevertheless take account of them."

How can one simultaneously live by "In God we trust, all others bring data" and "The most important figures. . . are unknown or unknowable. . ." simultaneously? They seem mutually exclusive. One way is to be rigorous about gathering the data that is available while acknowledging that some decisions need to be made without a full understanding of the potential consequences. A good example would be taking preventive action for a product design flaw based on lab testing during the development phase. What data is available?
- The lab test data certainly.
- Likely also FMEA or related analyses.
- Maybe information on similar products.

What data is not available?
- Whether the problem would have occurred in the field had the design not been improved. One can argue that this is a given based

28

on the completed analyses, but lab testing is an imperfect simulation of actual use in the field.

- Assuming the problem would have occurred, to what extent?
  - What percentage of the products would have exhibited the problem?
  - How expensive would the problem have been?
    - Warranty repairs.
    - Lost business due to customer dissatisfaction.
    - Liability if the problem resulted in injury.
  - What opportunity costs would have been lost because of resources being committed to fixing this preventable problem?

Certainly, we need to gather the data to determine whether this potential problem is likely enough and serious enough to warrant preventive action. Also, we should gather whatever data we can to estimate the potential costs. We can even estimate some of the "unknowable" information such as lost business due to customer dissatisfaction. Ultimately, we need to realize the necessity of making a decision based on an incomplete understanding of the risk.

I don't want to give the false impression that instinct or intuition have no place in Quality Engineering. It might seem incongruous given the theme of this section, but I have found instinct or intuition to be extremely valuable. There have been times when some idea or discussion has just "felt wrong", leaving me uneasy even though I could not at the time verbalize why. In those instances, it has proven invaluable to delay the decision and look for the data that would either confirm the feeling or provide confidence in the decision and alleviate the feeling of unease. Sometimes further investigation has uncovered adequate information to support the initial decision despite the misgiving; other times there was a flaw in the original justification that would have caused unacceptable expense had the idea been implemented.

It is those latter instances that prove the value of "intuition". In fact, I've found the most effective engineers or managers are those that understand a topic so well that they can tell at a glance when something looks wrong – even if it requires digging or further analysis to verbalize/explain why. Some of my most momentous decisions started with a feeling of "there has to be a better way" or "something isn't quite right".

4 Maintaining Credibility

Quality professionals often have to deliver bad news, whether related to machine downtime, scrap, customer complaints, QMS audit findings, or for a myriad of other reasons. Too often this need to deliver bad news can undermine the credibility of the Quality professional. People might walk the other way when the Quality Engineer comes down the hall or talk over her in meetings. Quality personnel can get a Chicken Little "the sky is falling" reputation. This chapter deals with gaining and maintaining credibility in general, not only when delivering bad news. Personal attributes such as competence and integrity require constant vigilance to maintain and enhance.

In a 1990s-leadership seminar, the instructor asked that we finish the following "trust is like. . .". After thinking for a while one response became obvious to me. "Trust is like a tree, it takes a long time to grow but only a moment to cut down". A high level of trust is never more important than when delivering bad news. Imagine the response if the one delivering the bad news has a reputation for exaggeration, show-boating, always being pessimistic, or worse yet dumping problems for others to fix and then disappearing.

Fortunately, the Quality professional has primary control over how she is viewed by others. Certain behaviors/traits can enhance her credibility. Conversely, different behaviors/traits will hasten the loss of credibility. The behaviors below tend to retain or enhance credibility.

Be objective and treat everyone the same. A belief that "the rules apply to everyone except Quality" is quite damaging to credibility. I've had to report to Management on the progress of many projects over the years. For some of those projects it has been most useful to send out a weekly update listing tasks that are due soon or overdue. The overdue tasks are in red text to make the information easier to digest at a glance. **My name has been in red text many times over those years.** It can be tough to send out an e-mail essentially stating that you have not met commitments. However, maintaining objectivity and fairness requires this. I've even listed my boss's name in red text as being late. This presents a whole different set of concerns, many of which center around the type of boss one has. I'd suggest a careful approach to listing one's boss in red text as being late. It's a good idea to at least give her or him a heads up to avoid an unpleasant surprise. With certain bosses, it could be career-limiting to list their name in red text. The best managers will understand the importance of credibility and support completely objective reporting even if it points at them as late with a deliverable. Unfortunately, not everyone has the luxury of working for this type of manager.

Rather than just reporting a problem and walking away, be part of the solution.

- If a customer found nonconforming product, lead the Root Cause Analysis and Corrective Action effort or at minimum offer ideas to help solve the problem.
- If there is a compliance problem with a QMS procedure (CAPA anyone?), volunteer to re-write the procedure and make it easier for the user.
- If uncertainty about criteria is causing excessive scrap, volunteer to lead the effort to clarify the criteria.
- If machine downtime is excessive, can you help by leading root cause analysis?
- Can you lead or help with scrap reduction efforts? Many Quality tools are uniquely suited to problem solving.

Don't minimize the situation, but as much as possible focus on the positives. Definitely, don't exaggerate on the negative side.

- Use objective data whenever possible.
- State conclusions based on facts. Leave opinions out of the presentation or, if an opinion is necessary, clearly identify it as such.
- Acknowledge uncertainties in data as well as possible alternative conclusions.
- Avoid hidden agendas!

- If a customer is dissatisfied with a specific corrective action, don't turn this into a condemnation of the CAPA system even though it might be in dire need of overhaul. The customer dissatisfaction can be a piece of supporting evidence that a CAPA system overhaul is needed, but by itself is not adequate to cast a shadow over the entire system.
- If people suspect a hidden agenda, they will spend more time trying to find alternate meanings than they will considering any proposed solution being offered.
- Don't use an external audit to promote your agenda. At lead auditor training, the instructor told stories about auditees pointing out deficiencies to the auditor so they would be recorded as findings and corrected. While some may consider such a tactic "successful" since the problem gets corrected, the loss of credibility and/or generating a reputation of undermining the company will hinder or destroy future success. There are much more effective ways at getting problems corrected.
- Don't propose a solution that makes your job easier but overall adds cost for the company. In fact, if a decision will make your job easier you would be well served to spend extra time reviewing your motives and ensuring that decision is best for the company. I've heard the accusation multiple times over the years that "the rules apply to everyone except Quality". Sometimes this is an attempt to deflect the issue by the person making the statement, other times it has caused me to re-think, and on occasion reverse, a decision that in hindsight might have made Quality's job easier but not been in the best interests of the company as a whole.
- Only state conclusions based on facts, leave opinions out of it or, if opinion adds value, be sure to identify it as an opinion rather than implying or allowing others to assume it is fact-based.

Admit mistakes. I hate being wrong and work very hard, double-check work, etc. to avoid this. Mistakes still happen. It is difficult to admit a mistake, but credibility absolutely requires that you do so.

Quality is typically in the approval loop for documents created at a business – from procedures and work instructions to engineering reports, inspection records, and many others. Carefully consider when sending someone else's work back for correction. Do you really want to spend $2000.00 and 3 weeks of time to disapprove a document just to fix th single typo in this sentence? Maybe, depending on the use of the document - some documents are important enough to demand perfection. Often, a simple typo can be fixed in the next revision without any risk or, if the procedure allows, can be fixed without re-submitting for formal approval. It bothers me to let typos like this go, but I have on occasion forced myself to do so. Consider that the author of a given document may have many hours invested in its creation, have many other tasks to accomplish, and the document may have been already reviewed and approved by multiple reviewers, sometimes including customers. The disapproval/rejection then requires rework by everyone involved to date and might result in missing a deadline. The perfectionist side of me is having a hard time writing this paragraph, however I believe it contributes to one's overall success. I worked with someone who had a reputation for rejecting documents multiple times for a single, simple typo. While everyone respected her knowledge, people avoided her to the point where it reduced her effectiveness. One must be **very** careful accepting typos in this fashion. Specifically, if there is **any reasonable** possibility that the typo could result in a misinterpretation of the sentence it must be corrected – especially if that misinterpretation could affect the quality of a product or service. It seems pretty obvious that, despite the intentional typo, the intent of the earlier sentence is apparent and there is no chance of misinterpretation resulting in any negative consequences. Caution: I've had others interpret something I wrote as a typo and "fix" it with good intentions. They did not understand the terms/concepts and unintentionally changed the meaning. Please don't make this mistake.

As hinted at earlier, integrity is essential to credibility. Due to the nature of the job, this is more apparent in the Quality profession than others. Specifically, since Quality professionals are given extensive approval/disapproval authority, a reputation for capriciousness, vindictiveness, favoritism, or selfishness will destroy credibility and effectiveness. One excellent method for avoiding the negative reputation and maintaining credibility is to make principle-based decisions (see chapter 2). Details regarding the principles may differ depending on type of business, but defining and acting upon a stable set of principles will put you firmly on the path of maintaining credibility.

The need for credibility goes beyond a person's employer and extends to customers, suppliers, regulators, among others. One particular example stands out. We had a Japanese customer who was finding nonconforming product. At the time, my employer was suffering a downturn in business and people were worried about a layoff. Our investigation found that when we had rejected product internally for sorting, the employees doing the sorting viewed the task as "busy work" and were less than diligent about finding and removing the nonconforming product, resulting in multiple escapes to the customer. This prompted the customer to visit our facility to discuss these nonconformances. I told the Plant Manager to whom I reported that no other explanation made sense and these customers were astute enough to see through any other explanation. Although the truth was embarrassing to both of us and we were reluctant to have that discussion, I told her it was likely we would need to 'fess up'. We mutually agreed to see how the conversation went before deciding to bring this up.

During the visit, it became apparent the customer knew we were holding back so the Plant Manager, via a nod, gave me approval to be open with them. The change in the meeting was almost immediate. The customer agreed that what we told them fit the facts of the case and thanked us for being open even though the subject was rather embarrassing. How does this relate to credibility? My personal credibility with that customer was extremely high for as long as I worked in that job. That customer would even call me years later when they questioned the thoroughness or validity

35

of responses they received from Quality Engineers working in a different division at my employer. They would ask me to review the information and, only after I told them it was accurate and thorough, did they accept the response. I did have to push the QE in the other division to be more thorough than their initial response to the customer and this thoroughness was essential to maintaining the credibility, both personal and for the organization.

Last, but clearly not least, become and remain competent in the Quality disciplines! I "grew up" in industry back in the 1980s. Back then, Quality in some circles had a reputation for being the department where people were assigned if they didn't have the formal education or capability to be successful in the Engineering department. This has changed dramatically for the better over the past 30 years, but still might linger in some industries. Why is this even mentioned? The reputation was created at least in part by Quality professionals who did not strive to improve their competency in the discipline. This paragraph should go without saying, but anything that "goes without saying" is worth saying explicitly so it isn't slowly, and over time, forgotten. Reference chapter 9 for related information.

Don't repeat the myths listed in this book. I had a customer once argue basic trigonometry with me. The customer representative wasn't an engineer and didn't seem to understand the trig, yet tried to bluff his way through the debate.

I remember another debate with a customer that requires a little more explanation. I was at the customer site explaining a problem using a simple lever arm (moment arm) argument. Again, the customer representative was not a trained engineer and didn't believe my explanation. He was so sure of his argument that he called me into a conference room with two engineers from his customer to whom the parts were eventually sold. Since these two **were** trained engineers, they listened to the explanation, quickly told me it made logical/engineering sense and properly explained the problem. I can't imagine this did

36

anything to improve the reputation/credibility of the representative who challenged the engineering explanation.

Fortunately, correcting any gap in professional competence is in our control. Even without a college degree, there are many ways to become and remain competent. A great example is by obtaining an American Society for Quality (ASQ) certification. ASQ offers certifications in many different focus areas within the Quality field such as Quality Engineer, Quality Manager, Six Sigma Black Belt, Reliability Engineer, etc. Go to asq.org and examine the BOK (Body Of Knowledge) for a quick overview. There are many very good seminars and training courses, some on-line, to develop and maintain professional competency. If we want to be credible, we must be able to help others when they have questions related to the Quality discipline. We must be able to provide the right answer at the right time across a wide range of topics. The only way to do this consistently is to study the discipline.

5 Worst Possible Answer

I often ask a specific question during training sessions. **What is the worst possible answer to any question?** Typical responses include:
- The wrong one
- An answer that costs a lot of money
- An answer we don't like
- One that creates a lot of work

The worst possible answer to any question is one that is "wrong but believable". Believable means we will take action based on the answer. Wrong means we'll take the wrong action. Wrong actions can have consequences ranging from a little wasted time to loss of life. The best answer obviously is the right one.

This was impressed on me while working on a diagnostic medical device. The risk assessment identified "wrong but believable" as much worse than just "wrong". Incorrectly indicating disease could result in (in this case risky) improper treatment. Incorrectly indicating lack of disease could result in failure to treat a serious condition. In either case, the wrong answer needs to be believable for someone to take the wrong action. If the answer is clearly wrong, the doctor will simply not believe the measurement and find a different way to make the diagnosis. Obvious failure of the equipment can present a hazard in itself, but providing a wrong but believable answer magnifies the potential negative effects.

A few examples might be useful:
- If a doctor believes a patient has high blood pressure when in reality it's fine, she will be tempted to write a prescription for unnecessary medication. Conversely if the doctor believes blood pressure is fine when it is really high, it will remain untreated and the patient will continue to have elevated risk of related complications. Consider now a blood pressure reading that is so wrong the doctor does not believe it to be accurate. In this latter case, the doctor will simply take another reading with a different piece of equipment and then make the correct decision.

- The first time I tried to give blood in high school I was deferred for high blood pressure. In the doctor's office, it again measured high. Although the blood pressure was higher than desired, it was within a treatable and hence believable range. Fortunately, my doctor questioned the reading in an otherwise healthy high school student and re-measured blood pressure after I had been allowed to chill out for a while. Result: "white coat hypertension". At that time, my blood pressure would spike when nervous. Giving blood for the first time was a little intimidating and sitting in the doctor's office after being deferred didn't help. 40 years later I'm still giving blood and my blood pressure is still within normal bounds without medication. Prescribing blood pressure medication to someone without high blood pressure can cause unnecessary health problems.

- A number of years ago, my wife had a positive medical test that implied ovarian cancer. To make matters worse, a Google search indicated that a positive test accompanied by physical symptoms correlated to a 90%+ chance of cancer. 6-weeks and a major surgery later we found out this was a false positive. Wrong, but believable in this case led to weeks of unnecessary worry and a surgery that might not have been required had the test not led to an incorrect diagnosis. Would a different treatment have been chosen if the doctor had better information? We'll never know.

- Back in the realm of business decisions, wrong but believable data could result in:
  - Incorrectly buying a new piece of equipment because we thought it outperformed the current equipment
  - Scrapping, sorting, or reworking product because a measurement was written down incorrectly
  - Choosing a supplier with worse quality because initial testing indicated the new supplier had quality at least comparable to that of the current supplier
  - Failing a validation because of measurement error
  - Erroneously rejecting the equivalence of two processing methods (type I error)

- o Erroneously accepting the equivalence of two processing methods (type II error)
- Regular monitoring indicated that our measurement systems are providing wrong answers. However, it's odd that all measurement systems "went bad" at the same time. On the other hand, it's odd that all parts used for monitoring "went bad" at the same time. This happened at a previous employer. I had to make a decision – believe the monitoring method and shut down all of production on a weekend or believe the measurement systems and keep running. As this happened on a weekend in high-volume manufacturing, it was a high 6-figure to low 7-figure decision. There were significant arguments in either direction. The procedure said to shut down and this would have been the easy decision given the data that was initially available. Gathering more data, over the course of only a few hours given the urgency of a decision, resulted in a decision to keep running. This decision was confirmed the next day by having monitoring parts shipped from a different site that was manufacturing similar product. In this case, the conclusion provided by the original monitoring parts was clearly believable – their only function after all was to tell us when the measurement systems failed. That conclusion, however, was wrong and only diligent consideration of all available data resulted in the correct action.
- Customer complaints are almost always believable. In the service industry however, sometimes the customer is the source of the problem rather than the employee being complained about. One should ask if the complaint represents a pattern before disciplining or "re-training" the employee. Conversely, effusive praise for a given employee might be insincerely provided by the employee's relative.

Interestingly, the week I'm writing this chapter (May, 2017) the FDA announced a recall for a product that "may underestimate the blood lead levels (BLL) and give inaccurate results when processing venous blood samples. Falsely lower test results may lead to improper patient management and treatment for lead exposure or poisoning. The use of

40

affected product may cause serious adverse health consequences." Many other diagnostic tests have worse consequences if wrong than those for lead levels. A quick review of FDA recalls over the previous year identified 4 additional recalls related to "wrong but believable" information.

Statistical analysis is particularly prone to "wrong but believable" answers. Consider the data set below. It's re-created from an occurrence rather early in my career. The customer required each lot of 3000 parts be sampled and the Cpk to be greater than 1.0 for the lot to be shipped. Rework was not possible and sorting not cost-effective; the only two dispositions were to ship or scrap. The results, at a glance, were believable. Occasionally, although not often, our process would create a group of parts that would measure as indicated and need to be scrapped. I was responsible for approving any scrap disposition. I looked at the numbers for about 20 seconds and told the QC Auditor that I thought she entered the data incorrectly. She looked at me like I was crazy, not believing that anyone can calculate the standard deviation of 50 numbers in their head. She was right, hopefully not about me being crazy, but about me not being able to calculate standard deviation in my head. Can you, in 20 seconds, see what I did that led to the conclusion?

Tolerance: 0 +/- 0.5

0.25	0.17	0.06	0.37	0.17
0.41	0.12	0.28	0.23	0.15
0.17	0.21	0.29	0.10	0.18
0.17	0.28	0.04	0.21	0.16
0.16	0.26	0.18	0.13	0.27
0.24	0.13	0.22	0.25	0.06
0.20	0.19	0.09	0.22	0.09
0.12	0.32	0.20	0.15	0.36
0.17	0.17	0.20	0.11	0.22
0.18	0.19	0.24	0.10	0.32

Average:	0.20
Standard Deviation:	0.5525
Cpk:	0.184

Figure 5.1 – Data Entry Error

The smallest measurement is 0.04 and the largest 0.41. Range is easily calculated to be 0.37. The standard deviation is listed as 0.55. It's mathematically impossible for 1 standard deviation of a given data set to be larger than the range of that same data set. What's the most plausible cause of the error? Manually entering 4.1 instead of the correct value of 0.41 – a simple decimal point error. Correcting this error results in a Cpk of 1.27 and 3000 parts shipped rather than scrapped. For one who understands the math behind the statistics, this "trick" is straightforward. For one who lacks the mathematical understanding, it's more like black magic. Note: Ppk would be more appropriate in this instance than Cpk. Reference chapter 28 for more explanation of this. The actual example occurred before Ppk came into common use.

How best can we deal with the wrong but believable problem?
- If you are a QE or RE, study the discipline to be good at it.

- If you are a manager, hire competent people and provide the necessary training and support to help them become and remain competent.
- Understand the science and math behind the tools and use them appropriately.
    - Science and math don't cease being relevant when you are awarded the piece of paper stating you completed a college degree. To the contrary, that's when they really mean something. A degree is worthless unless the knowledge it represents is used to solve real world problems.
    - Particularly with statistics, understanding the math behind it helps avoid the "wrong but believable" problem by reducing the size of the "believable" range. Over time, a good QE will develop such an understanding of the math behind some of the statistics as to develop an "intuition" wherein the analysis looks wrong. This feeling then prompts a closer look, eventually leading to the identification/correction of the error.

SPC (Statistical Process Control) was created to prevent a problem similar to the "wrong but believable" situation. SPC is used to distinguish between a true change and random variation. If the part we have in front of us measured larger than the previous part measured, it might be because something in the process changed – machine settings, operator, material lot, etc. or it might be simple random variation. Both answers, true change or random variation, are believable. One is right, the other wrong. SPC was developed to help us figure out which answer is correct. Rarely will any two consecutive measurements be exactly the same; there is variation in everything. If the most recent measurement is higher (lower) than the previous, should we take action to correct the process? In this case the data is correct, the conclusion about the cause can be wrong. The costs of ignoring a problem are easily recognized by most in business; the costs of acting to fix a non-existent problem are not as easily recognized. It can be shown that reacting to every measurement can actually increase variation and reduce the quality of a product.

Consider the X-bar and R control chart in figure 5.2. The data is simulated from a normal distribution. Through point 25, the process is allowed to run uninterrupted. At point 26, the data are modified to simulate an operator trying to adjust every point to nominal. For example, point 25 is approximately 0.3 units above nominal (assume "25" is nominal). The result for point 26 is then adjusted by -0.3 units before being plotted. Point 26 is approximately 2.1 units below nominal, so point 27 is adjusted by +2.1 units before being plotted, etc. This is similar to Dr. Deming's funnel experiment and analogous to the operator trying to adjust the process "back to nominal" every time a measurement is taken. Making unnecessary adjustments to a process that is running in control is referred to as "over-adjusting" or "tweaking". A few observations are in order:

- The Operator making the adjustments in the simulation almost certainly has good intentions – why wouldn't we want every part as close to nominal as possible?
- Changing the symbols on the graphs to squares is Minitab's way of indicating an ooc (out of control) point. The small numbers by the squares indicate which of the control chart rules have been violated.
- The process is quite well behaved through point 25 - that is, in a state of statistical control. We did experience one point slightly out of control on the MR (Moving Range) chart. That will happen on occasion due to random chance and, since we know the data is from a normal distribution, this is a false signal.
- Adjusting a process that is in control increases variation and eventually forces it out of control as indicated by the chart.
- "Adjusting to nominal" when a process is in control will result in increasing oscillations around the nominal value.
- Notice that while the over-adjusting commenced at point 26, the first out of control signal was indicated 2 points later, at point 28, but that's only if all out of control rules are being followed. Many companies only use the first rule (a point beyond the 3-sigma control limits. If only using this first rule, the first out of control signal on the X-chart happens 8 points later, at point 34. The MR chart does send an out of control signal at point 27, only 1 point

44

after the overadjustment commenced. In my experience, more attention is placed on the X-chart and this point may or may not have sparked an investigation.

- The operator who started the over-adjusting may believe he is receiving positive feedback on his efforts; points 29 – 33 for example are all close to nominal.
- The delay before the control chart goes out of control could easily span shifts/crews. That is, the operator who make the improper adjustments might never see the effects on the chart – the out-of-control condition might not show up until the next crew.
- This delay is likely to result in a wrong conclusion about the reason the process went out of control – after all, the process appeared to improve (or at least not get worse) when the over-adjustments started.
- Similar to the wrong but believable answer, preventing this type of error simply requires an understanding and application of the math and theory behind the situation.
- I've run many simulations of this sort. While in this case ooc rules were triggered quite early, in other simulations the process can seem to be stable or even show slight improvement for 10 or more samples before the erratic behavior starts.

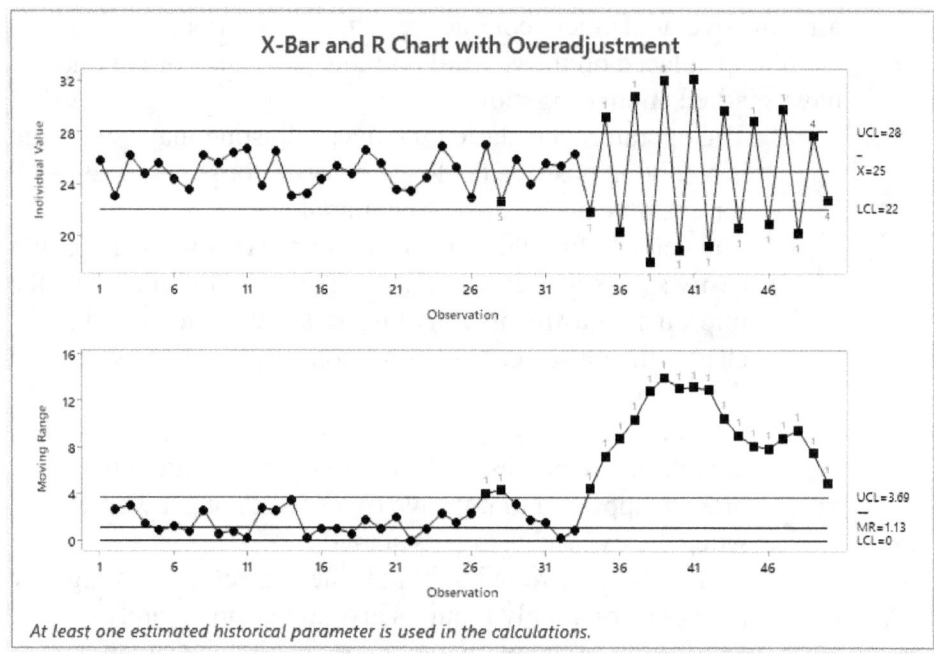

Figure 5.2 – Control Chart Exhibiting Over-Adjustment

6 Most Important part of a QMS (Quality Management System) or a Quality Manual

What is the most important part of a QMS or Quality Manual? This question has sparked some very interesting discussions.

Major portions of a QMS include [ISO 13485:2016]:
- Documentation/Records
- Customer Focus
- Quality Policy
- Management Commitment
- Planning
- Responsibility, Authority and Communication
- Management Review
- Provision of Resources
- Human Resources
- Infrastructure
- Work Environment and Contamination Control
- Planning of Product Realization
- Customer-Related Processes
- Design and Development
- Purchasing
- Production and Service Provision
- Control of Monitoring and Measuring Equipment
- Monitoring and Measurement
- Control of Nonconforming Product
- Analysis of Data
- Improvement

Strong argument can be made for many of these.
- Proper documentation is required to consistently manufacture the same product

- o Unclear drawings will be interpreted differently by different people and the interpretation is subject to change over time.
  - o Inadequate control of drawing revisions will result in some product being manufactured to an old revision.
  - o Quality records are required by regulation in many industries. Failure to maintain adequate records subjects a company to possible legal action – fines and/or lawsuits.
  - o Is Documentation then the most important part?
- A product company lives by developing and marketing new products.
  - o Design and Development is a core competency for such a company and the company will fail in the absence of good systems for this activity.
  - o Is Design and Development then the most important for such a company?
- A manufacturing company is successful only if it can manufacture competitive product – quality, price, service.
  - o Is Production and Service Provision then the most important portion for such a company?
- "If you can't measure it, you can't improve it." [Peter Drucker]
  - o Is Monitoring and Measurement then the most important?
- Experience has shown that one section not yet mentioned outweighs all others. What section is that? **Management commitment.** Consider:
  - o Regarding documentation, what if:
    - ▪ The company president is asking employees to work to uncontrolled memos, sticky notes, etc.
    - ▪ The staffing and timelines are such that there are not adequate resources to provide proper updating and control of engineering drawings
    - ▪ In contrast, envision a scenario where the President consistently reinforces the idea that work will only be done as directed in properly controlled Work Instructions (WIs) and enforces this policy, not only

in Manufacturing where the work is done, but also in Engineering where the WIs are created.

- o Regarding Design and Development:
    - Are proper design reviews likely to happen if Management considers them to be a waste of time?
    - FEA (Finite Element Analysis) is often required for proper stress/strength analysis. The technique is complicated and requires sophisticated software. Management has to decide whether or not to approve the expense to invest in the software and in trained individuals to use it properly.
    - Which is more likely to be successful?
        - A scenario wherein Management hires personnel without the proper training, neglects or refuses to provide adequate training, yet expects world-class product development.
        - A Management team that identifies necessary skills, hires people trained in those skills and/or provides adequate training, and provides the tools (software, etc.) required to properly do the job.
- o Consider Production and Service Provision
    - There is often pressure to improve speed/efficiency and meet deadlines. This is necessary and desirable. Only Management can create and promote a culture that maintains quality at the same time as meeting these objectives. Contrarily, Management could take any number of actions that would, maybe unintentionally, undermine the efforts to produce a quality product.
- o Measurement of product is undeniably important
    - Consider a scenario wherein a CMM (Coordinate Measuring Machine) is required for accurate measurements, but the capital is never approved and the only tool provided is a tape measure.

- Management approves the budget and capital purchases. The above example is somewhat extreme (although not as much as it may seem), but the basic principle is that Management approval is required to provide necessary tools to perform the job.

I was recently challenged that 'everyone is responsible for quality and the premise of this chapter removes responsibility from the bulk of the employees. The rebuttal is easy – who (role) creates and fosters a quality culture within which every employee feels responsible for quality? Only management can foster such a culture consistently.

It is easy to show that Management Commitment is necessary for any portion of a QMS to be successful. By extension then, Management Commitment is the most important part of a QMS. There can be small victories in the absence of adequate Management Commitment, but truly creating a culture of quality can only be done with active involvement and promotion by Management, specifically Executive Management.

7 Myth: "We know we've shipped this condition before and the customer hasn't complained, so they must view it as acceptable."

Reality:
The customer may have seen the condition but decided not to react to the low level of escapes. If we suddenly accept the condition and send more parts with it, the customer backlash may be such that even the low level of escapes occurring previously are now raised to the level of a major concern.

The customer may have not yet seen the condition but may react differently than expected when they notice it. If this hasn't happened to you, it may seem unlikely. In reality, it is a fairly common occurrence. What types of events can bring a previously overlooked condition to the attention of a customer?

- A new inspector finds it. The fact that it has existed previously does **not** make it acceptable once found.
- Problems in the customer's manufacturing process are traced back to the previously overlooked condition.
- The condition caused latent field failures.
- Etc.

Another possibility is that the condition may be at the limit of acceptability. If we now assume it is acceptable and change our criteria, what if it gets worse? Where is the new limit of acceptability? As time goes along, this could become an instance of normalization of deviance as described in chapter 2.

The customer may have seen the condition but decided to deal with the low level without filing a complaint or notifying the supplier. When might this happen? It might occur if the condition cannot make it through the customer's process and the cost of reworking or yield loss is so small that it doesn't rank high enough on the Pareto. Imagine now if the supplier decides the condition is acceptable and begins sending a majority of product with that condition. What was a minor annoyance to the customer immediately moves to or near the top of the Pareto. The response to this event is often such that, not only is the current situation unacceptable, but the previous low level of escapes is no longer acceptable. The assumption that "because the customer hasn't complained, the condition is acceptable" often results in tighter criteria, lower yield, more downtime, and higher cost going forward. **I've found through my career that one of the quickest ways to get a customer to tighten criteria is to consistently send them marginal product, even if technically acceptable.**

The above description was developed with attribute criteria in mind - pass/fail, go/no-go, or visual. An analogy with variable data is explored in more detail in the next chapter.

The solution is rather simple. Either talk with the customer to develop a better understanding of the true acceptability limit or improve the process to no longer send the marginal or nonconforming product.

Another possibility exists – the issue had existed for quite some time and had simply gone unnoticed. I can recall many examples throughout my career, but one in particular stands out. I was discussing a supplier problem with a corporate VP. The problem had been going on for some time and had recently come to light. After some rather heated discussion, the VP made a statement along the lines of "The supplier has been doing it this way for years, what changed?". I thought for a few moments and replied "**I became aware**". We were working in a regulated industry and I could have placed myself in legal jeopardy by allowing the practice to continue. **There is a big difference between immediately addressing a problem once identified and continuing to knowingly promote poor practice.** This distinction is not clear to everyone – or some people may have motivation to act as if the distinction is not clear.

While it is impossible to go back in time and change the past, it is expected that we correct a problem **once it has been identified** – particularly if the problem carries ethical or legal considerations. A mistake is human; doing the same thing deliberately may be criminal.

8 Myth: As Long as All Parts Are Within Tolerance, the Actual Value Isn't Important.

Reality: Parts at nominal may perform better than parts near the tolerance limit.

In some cases, the "myth" is actually true. Envision a shaft that needs to fit into a hole without concern for location within that hole. If the tolerances on hole and shaft are set such that clearance is assured if both components are in tolerance, it is true that a part near the lower limit will work as well as a part at nominal or near the upper limit. There are many situations, however, where this does not hold. The remainder of this chapter deals with those instances where the myth is not true.

"As long as all parts are within tolerance, the actual value is not important" is a corollary to the myth in chapter 7. Consider a tolerance zone 10 units wide. If our process is capable of holding +/- 1 unit, we can make all conforming product with a process average shifted 8 units from nominal. Consider the possibility that while product 8 units from nominal is conforming, it may not work quite as well as one at nominal. For example, due to tolerance stack-ups it may be that a product at nominal is guaranteed to assemble properly while a product shifted by 8 units has a 3% chance of being rejected in the customer's process. If a small percentage of the products are actually shifted by 8 units, the fallout rate may never be noticed by the customer. However, if the distribution is shifted such that the average product is shifted by 8 units, the customer is likely to notice the resulting 3% defect rate. The likely outcome of consistently shipping product with an 8 unit mean shift? Tighter overall tolerance or a mean centering tolerance.

I started my Quality career working for a component manufacturer in the computer disk drive industry in the 80s. Readers may remember that during the 80s and 90s, rigid disk drive (RDD) capacity was increasing rapidly. This was often viewed as the RDD analog to Moore's Law in semiconductors. Areal density, or how much data can be packed into each square inch of a disk, is one measure used to quantify RDD capacity. Improving areal density required the read-write head to fly ever closer to the disk. Fly height was the term used for this.

Constantly reducing fly height required ever tightening tolerances on some of the components. The tolerances were constantly pushing state-of-the-art in manufacturing capability. That is, as soon as we developed good capability our customers would tighten tolerances. Components built to nominal had lower fly height than components built within tolerance, but close to the tolerance limit. This was not a simple clearance-fit situation. The component parameters contributed to fly height in a complex manner. I was involved in a situation wherein a particular lot of components were produced with a tighter than typical distribution, but this distribution was shifted near the upper tolerance. After considerable discussion, the lot was shipped to the customer – after all, every part met tolerance. This particular lot of parts caused problems in the customer's process. The parts were not returned since they all met tolerance, however a short time later the customer added a mean centering tolerance to the drawing. The mean centering tolerance required the mean of every lot to be within 10% of nominal (for example). While the tails were still allowed to approach the tolerance limits, a narrow, shifted distribution would not be accepted. Mean centering specifications became common in the industry.

Imagine a situation where the customer is highly concerned with process yield and the customer's process is sensitive to one or more component parameters. If the supplier has a history of producing consistent product, the customer's process will be adjusted or dialed in to maximize yield based on the historical component distribution. Imagine further in such a scenario that the supplier makes a change that results in a shifted distribution, even for a short period of time. The shifted distribution will cause lower yield at the customer and likely result in a customer complaint. Seem unlikely? Based on my experience this situation occurs more frequently than expected.

Both situations are illustrated graphically in figure 4. Imagine for the sake of simplicity that the yellow shaded areas on the graph indicate an area within the tolerance zone which results in a higher than desired likelihood of final assembly failure at the customer. It can be easily seen that the shifted distribution places many more components in this "danger zone" for yield loss than a centered distribution even if, and especially because, the shifted distribution is much narrower.

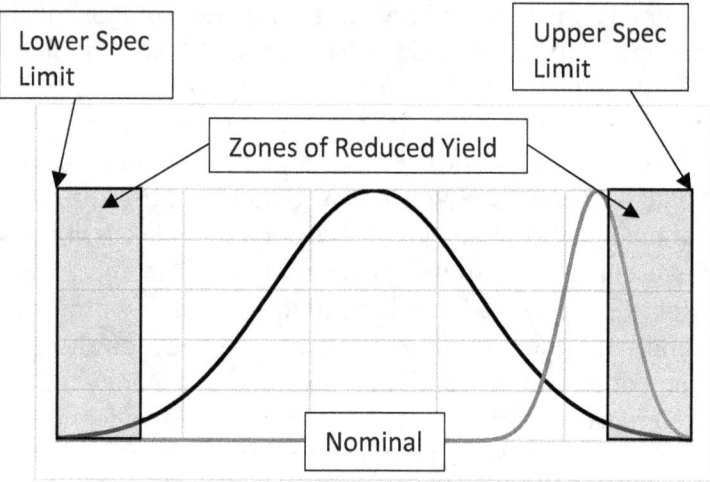

Figure 8.1 – Impact of Shifted Distribution

The above examples are specific manifestations of Taguchi's Loss Function.

9 Myth: Quality Is A Given, So We Don't Need to Talk About It Anymore.

Reality: What gets talked about receives priority.

This myth, like many other poor practices discussed in this book, is particularly insidious because it's rooted in good intentions. Every good business strives for a state wherein all employees are committed to delivering quality product or service, on time, to the customer. The myth might even be true for a short period of time – today, a few months, or years. The problem is if we actually implement the statement, i.e. stop talking about quality, over time it will naturally lose importance.

Consider an employee who is asked multiple times every day how many parts were produced, how many customers were served, how many calls were completed, how many invoices were sent, how many injections were given, etc. Now consider that the same employee is not asked, or is rarely asked, about how good the parts were, the satisfaction level of the customers, the error rate on invoices, the number of injections that had to be repeated due to error, etc. Consider further that employee meetings contain a similar focus. After all, why talk about Quality when everyone knows it's priority #1? Even further, consider that employee performance and merit increases are dependent upon the same factors that are given all of the attention in daily interactions and company meetings. Would it be a surprise then to find that the priority placed on quality measures slowly degrades over time? I would assert rather that this degradation of quality is the **expected**, rather than surprising, result! It's what people hear every day or multiple times a day that has the largest influence on their behavior – not what they hear monthly, quarterly, or yearly. This seems a good time to remind readers that 80+% of problems are in management's control, not in the control of the employees (reference writings by W. Edwards Deming and Joseph Juran). A manager who uses quality to berate employees is not a good manager. Talking about quality needs to focus on fixing the process, not the person.

There is a reason why industry standards such as ISO 13485 require that management regularly communicate Quality Policy, Objectives, and Indicators/Results to all employees. It's because when we don't, people tend to forget about them or they naturally lose priority.

10 Myth: 'Quality Is Free', Therefore We Do Not Need to Invest Money In Quality Improvements.

Reality: This myth seems wrong at face value, yet I had a manager use the exact argument to deny funding for a project. While to this day I believe he had an ulterior motive rather than ignorance for making the comment, the rationale he provided for the decision would imply he meant what he said. The real meaning of 'Quality Is Free' is that quality improvements typically have good ROI (Return On Investment) and save more than they cost.

Typical savings from quality improvement activities:
- Improved equipment up-time/utilization
- Higher yields
- Improved efficiency/less time spent dealing with problems
- Improved customer satisfaction/increased revenue
- Increased market share
- Reduced accident/injury rate
- Lower complaint rate
- Lower warranty costs
- Fewer returns
- Improved employee satisfaction

As discussed in chapter 3, Dr. Deming stated that some of the most important information is unknown and unknowable. This can add difficulty to cost justification of quality improvement efforts. How can we put a cost on potential lost business when we cannot know if failure to improve a given condition will actually cause customers to leave? Questions such as this may make cost justification more challenging, but are no excuse for failure to try. Enlightened management will have a method to factor this type of consideration into funding/priority decisions for improvement projects. The details regarding how to factor in these considerations will be specific to each business.

11 Myth: The job of a Quality Inspector/Auditor is to find problems/defects.

Reality: The job of a Quality Inspector/Auditor is to find and report the truth. It's that simple and that important.

A different, but similar myth is that the job is to accept product.

Consider the likely outcome if a QI (Quality Inspector) views her job as finding nonconformities. The QI's will be tempted to track their job performance by the number of problems/defects/nonconformances found, with a larger number being better. It is logical in such a scenario that the QI will be tempted to interpret subjective criteria in the strictest manner possible – or at least in a stricter manner than intended. Consequences from this would include:
- lower yield
- unnecessary time spent sorting/reworking
- higher lot (false) failure rate
- increased conflict between the QI and Manufacturing
- wasted time trying to fix artificially created "problems"
- etc.

Stories about "quotas" for tickets in local police departments is an example of this type of thinking outside the business world. While the stories might not be true in many cases, the prevalence of them provides an indication of the potential for this thinking.

Alternatively, consider the likely outcome if a QI views his job as first, accepting product and second, failing only when the evidence is clear/overwhelming. In this case, it is logical that the QI will track job performance by lot passrate with a higher number being desired and thus interpret subjective criteria in the loosest manner possible. Consequences from this would include:
- increased customer complaints

- increased returns
- increased field failures
- increased hazards/reduced safety
- a failure to fix problems in a timely manner
- potentially lost customers/reputation
- etc.

I worked in a company where the QIs believed if they found "the only" nonconformance in the lot they were doing everyone a favor by replacing it and accepting the lot. Of course, they never "found the only one" since they only examined a small sample of the parts, but assumed they did because they had come to believe their job was to accept product unless the evidence became overwhelming to the contrary. Interestingly, this tendency was identified by examination of a frequency histogram of the number of lots with 0, 1, 2, etc. nonconformances. The frequency of 0 and 2 nonconformances was too large and the frequency of 1 nonconformance too small to be consistent with statistical theory. A QE who reported to me told the Inspectors that they would be more likely to be struck by lightning than for the sampling to be accurate and fortunately he had enough credibility with the QIs that they admitted to him what was really happening. This example is illustrated in figure 11.1. The data are fabricated for this example (I don't remember the specifics), so the y-axis is suppressed to show the concept without misleading/inaccurate details.

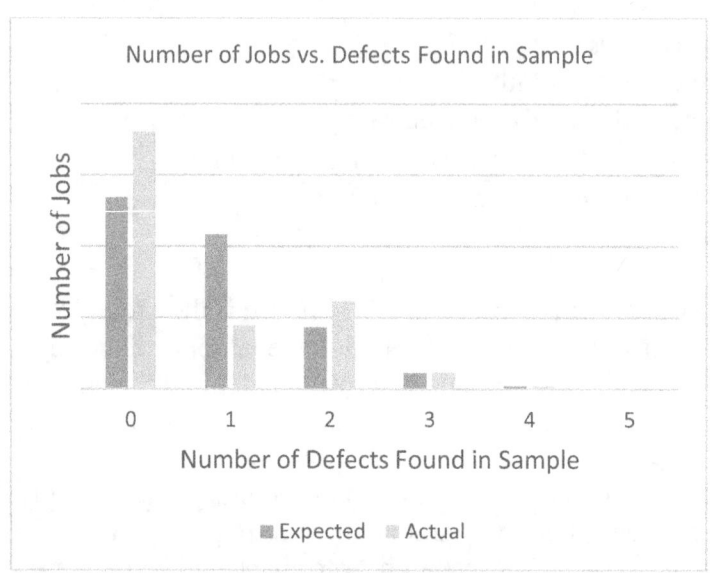

Figure 11.1 – Expected vs. Actual Number of Jobs vs. Number of Defects Found in Sample

Only in the case where a QI views her job as finding and reporting the truth can business performance be optimized. Only in this case can we be confident that our resources are truly spent fixing the most pressing problems and that the data generated from Quality audits can be trusted.

A Quality Auditor (QA) can audit parts, a process, or the QMS. The discussion for a part auditor is identical to the QI. The discussion for a QMS auditor is analogous. A QMS auditor that views his job as finding nonconformances will feel pressured to "write up" something even if the QMS under review is in full compliance. How many of us have had to respond to "findings" that in reality did not violate the standard? This practice over time results in a requirements creep and eventually companies can be held to requirements that don't exist in the standard. Over time, these superfluous requirements cause the QMS to become less efficient, less effective, and ultimately can cause it to collapse under its own weight. If a QMS auditor views her job as providing a certification, she might be tempted to either overlook or minimize any findings (i.e. record a major as a minor). Again, only in the case of "find and report the truth" can we rest assured that resources are being used in the most productive manner.

12 Myth: Purchase price equals cost.

Reality: Issues arising from poor quality can dwarf purchase price. These issues include: lot failures and associated paperwork costs, rework, sorting costs, yield loss in-process, stock-outs, field failures resulting from low quality components, and engineering time trying to fix problems.

The previous paragraph introduced a fine, yet important, distinction. If a business uses the term "cost" when referring to purchase price, it is likely that business will confuse the two terms. They are very distinct. Purchase price refers to the dollar amount paid for each unit of product (or service). Cost includes:

- Purchase price
- Time spent managing a new supplier
- In Manufacturing industries, time spent qualifying a new part and/or supplier. This may include:
    - First article inspection
    - On-site audit of the supplier
    - Incoming inspection
- If parts fail, time and money is spent dealing with the failure. This could include any of the items below.
    - QE, Buyer, Design Engineer, Manufacturing Engineer, Procurement Engineer time spent to resolve the problem.
    - Sorting and/or rework.
    - In-process scrap.
    - Customer complaints.
    - Warranty costs.

Explicitly distinguishing between purchase price and cost will help a company avoid confusing the two terms, help that company consider all costs when making decisions, avoid negative impacts to company resources and customers, and ultimately increase the company's profits.

Example 12.1: A cost-conscious company bought a new piece of measurement equipment. The model chosen had a low purchase price. It

64

was only after it was installed that the company realized it was less capable than older equipment, might not be adequate to fulfill needs a few years out, and might need to be replaced due to capability long before its useful life ended. Low purchase price, high cost due to required early replacement.

If Purchasing finds a lower cost component from a new supplier, is there a mechanism to evaluate quality, service, technical support, delivery, etc.? Problems in any of these areas can and will quickly negate any savings in purchase price.

Most readers can probably point to an example in their experience where either a new supplier was chosen or a cheaper component selected and the change resulted in failures and scrap at incoming inspection or worse yet in manufacturing or in the field. This is often due to a Purchasing cost reduction target that neglects to consider the downstream costs of lower quality parts. Remember this example when you get to chapter 14 as it would fit as well in that chapter as in this one.

Purchase price ≢ Cost

13 The importance of why

Compliance with procedures and requests is better if people understand why those procedures exist and why requests are made. Employees have a strong desire to understand the reasons behind a decision or a procedure. If management doesn't provide the reason, many employees will come up with a plausible reason - that is often wrong and can be counterproductive. This might be best illustrated by a couple of examples.

Example 13.1: There may be times when a customer will agree to accept nonconforming product, maybe because they can sort or rework it in their process, maybe because they have determined that the nonconformance will not have a detrimental effect on the finished product, maybe because their need for the product is such that they would rather commit their own resources to correcting any issues than to accept a delay in shipment. When employees know that nonconforming product has been shipped, what will they choose to believe if they are not aware that the customer has approved shipment? Based on past experience, many employees will believe that "quality doesn't really matter" (or this particular defect doesn't matter), "they (management) aren't really serious about quality", or "a few defects are ok". The real danger of this is that when employees believe any of the quoted statements they have to create a new, internal standard to which they will work. Each employee will create a different personal standard and it will appear to management that the quality system is not working. If management does not understand the real reason for the breakdown, they will not be able to fix the problem.

Example 13.2: Employees might not understand that their signature indicates they have verified and are personally guaranteeing that the information is correct. Further, they may not understand that the signature is required based on multiple mistakes made in the past. Not knowing the reasons for the signature can easily result in it becoming a "rubber stamp" rather than the actual intended verification of information.

Example 13.3: A customer consigned material and requested that even though some of the parts may be considered nonconforming, all parts be processed so they could review them and determine the acceptability. This represented a significant departure from normal practice. The instructions were documented without the reasoning/justification from the customer. Result: night shift shut down the process because of uncertainty regarding the legitimacy/interpretation of the (documented) instructions. The night shift employees clearly had the best interests of the customer and the business in mind and intentions of doing the right thing. If the reason for the instruction had been shared, all expenses related to process downtime and communicating the reasons after the fact could have been avoided.

Example 13.4: Long pants are required for safety reasons. Dress code is communicated to employees, but not the reason for the requirement. This results in morale problems and wasted time when people try to change the policy by arguing that Capris are more stylish/professional than pajama pants or full-length leggings. This argument makes no sense if one understands that the reason for the requirement is safety, not style. Employees can and do get quite worked up over issues such as this.

Example 13.5: Manufacturing couldn't find 3 of 5 QEs on a given day and assumed they were taking advantage of a WFH (work from home) policy. In reality, one QE had changed desk location and Manufacturing simply didn't look in the correct place while another was WFH due to a COVID exposure.

Early in my career as a Quality Engineer, I regularly interacted with a peer who often complained about how the QA Auditors would take a long time to complete a simple request, would get it wrong, or would complain about having to do the request. My impression of the same QA folks is that they were competent, industrious, and pleasant to work with. I was confused how we could have such different impressions of the same people, so I spent some time observing. It was quickly apparent that the difference was simply a matter of treating the QA folks with respect. The QE who had difficulty working with QA would speak to them in a condescending manner, ridicule mistakes, command rather than request, and rarely if ever use the words "please" and "thank you". I had an honest respect for the QA Auditors, listened to their opinions and made changes as appropriate, asked for their help, tried to minimize embarrassment when mistakes were made, and always tried to remember "please" and "thank you". At the time, I hadn't spent much time pondering the nuances of personal interaction. Fortunately, my upbringing and experiences nurtured that respect for others. Respecting others made my job easier and more enjoyable as well as helping me to accomplish more than I could have otherwise.

How does this relate to "the importance of why"? In many ways, explaining the reasons behind decisions comes down to a matter of respect. Explaining comes naturally when one respects the people he is dealing with; it is a detail to be remembered and a burden otherwise.

One final thought on the topic. Understanding the reasons behind procedures and policies make it less likely for employees to make a mistake when presented with an unusual situation. Consider manufacture of a medical device. If employees have a basic understanding of the need for Risk Management and how their decisions can affect the customer, doctor or patient (maybe a family member), they are less likely to make an unapproved change thinking that "it won't make a difference anyway".

14 Incenting Counterproductive Behaviors

Businesses need metrics to track performance. The number and type of metrics used varies greatly. Choice of metrics often is not given the careful consideration it deserves and can result in incentives for behaviors that are damaging to a business. Some examples of such metrics are given below.

Example 14.1: Excess inventory is considered a waste. As such, the amount of inventory is often tracked and, more specifically, inventory turns are often used as a metric. Further, financial incentives for those people involved in buying, planning, and/or scheduling are often tied to inventory turns with higher turns resulting in higher rewards. There is, however, a dark side to inventory turns and that dark side would be stock-outs. Minimizing inventory lowers cost only to the point where manufacturing lines may be shut down from lack of stock to continue production. A single stock-out can cost much more than carrying a little extra inventory. The answer is to balance the inventory turns indicator with an indicator related to stock-outs and weight those indicators accordingly. The best inventory control system is one that minimizes inventory while preventing stock-outs. Higher inventory turns are great until we go line down, then they're not so great anymore.

Example 14.2: High passrate at QC/QA is a desirable indicator insofar as it is achieved by improving quality. It also can result in damaging behavior. QA/QC auditors can intentionally overlook or ignore legitimate failures either due to intimidation or a desire to "help out their co-workers". I've seen this happen multiple times at multiple companies. It can be insidious and difficult to prove. High QC passrate is good until we deliberately overlook nonconforming product, then it's not. This indicator is more difficult to balance than the previously discussed inventory turns. The primary method for balancing this indicator is to create a culture of quality wherein employees in all departments are continuously rewarded for bringing problems to light so they can be solved – as opposed to a culture that rewards short-term (i.e. daily) results, sometimes at the expense of long-term performance. Other methods to balance this indicator would include:

- Customer feedback. This indicator is objective, the primary problem being a time lag. It can sometimes take months for feedback to be provided by customers.
- Post-QC/QA audits conducted by an entity with less direct connection to Manufacturing. This indicator represents a non-value-added cost. It might be a necessary cost if the culture is not set up to consistently promote quality, but is less desirable than creation of a culture of quality.

Example 14.3: Yield is an important indicator to track. Improving yield by reducing the number of nonconforming units will make a business more profitable. Yield can also be improved by applying looser quality standards and accepting nonconforming product. Intentional acceptance of nonconforming product will make the yield indicator look better and improve short-term profits. Higher yield is good until we stop rejecting nonconforming product, then it's not. These "benefits" will last only until customers figure out what is going on. If customers accept the lower quality as unintentional, the response may range from the need to provide corrective action to possibly tighter requirements. If customers view the lower quality as deliberate, the loss in trust could easily result in a lost customer. Yield targets should always be balanced with a quality target.

Example 14.4: Heavy focus on short-term operating income without a balancing quality target has led companies astray. Miniscribe became infamous in the 1980s for shipping bricks as completed disk drives. How management thought this could be a successful strategy is beyond me, but one can only envision a focus on short-term profits at the expense of long-term viability. Source: http://articles.latimes.com/1989-09-13/business/fi-2051_1_massive-fraud.

Example 14.5: At a previous job, department managers were graded and rewarded on managing budget – a proper goal of any department manager. The problem is that the highest reward was reserved for those managers that came in more than 10% under budget. The incentive here is to "pad"

70

the budget so the manager knows she can successfully come in 10% under. Where would be the incentive in this case to submit an honest budget? That incentive would have to be internal to the manager's value system since clearly the incentive system encourages overestimating the budget. Consider that a best estimate guess is 50% likely to be a little over and 50% likely to be a little under. In such a case, would not most managers pad their budget a little to increase the odds of coming in under budget and getting a good review/reward? Is it in the company's best interest to encourage managers to submit unrealistically high budgets? In this case I told my boss it felt like being given a choice between being foolish or being dishonest – accurate budget would make a good performance rating nigh impossible and would be foolish. A padded budget would be dishonest. I was able to successfully negotiate a rating scale that reserved the highest rating/reward for an accurate budget – within +/- X%. The second highest rating was for coming in under budget by more than X% with lower ratings for spending more than X% above budget. The negotiated rating/reward method clearly provides more emphasis on accuracy than the original method, thus aligning department manager priorities with those of the company – accurately forecast and manage spending.

Example 14.6: From a colleague: A plant manager held weekly staff meetings at which department managers were to present charts showing progress to business goals. The charts were color coded – green meant goals being met, red not met. The plant manager gave very clear instructions that he wanted to see a "sea of green" at these meetings. His wish was granted through "selective" or "creative" reporting. As the reader can guess, many of the graphs had only a passing acquaintance with reality. Green indicators/graphs are good until they're misleading, then they're not.

Example 14.7: Many companies have a "use it or lose it" policy with respect to budgeting. How this often works is if a department doesn't use its allocated budget any given year, the budget for the following year is reduced by a like amount. Example: department budget for this year is $2M, the department only uses $1.8M so the budget for next year is

$1.8M. This policy encourages waste as many departments scramble at the end of the year to spend all of their allocated budget to "preserve or protect" the budget amount for next year. Would it not be better for the company if every department spent only what's necessary and reduced expenses whenever it made business sense?

Example 14.8: The Wells Fargo example in chapter 2 resulted from incenting counterproductive behavior. Setting aggressive sales targets as a requirement for employees to keep their jobs or to qualify them for bonuses incenting the creation of fake customer accounts. Opening new accounts is good until they become fraudulent, then it's not. Reference: Koren, James Rufus, "Banking giant to be fined $185M", Minneapolis Star/Tribune 9/9/16.

Example 14.9: Winning business is of obvious importance. A new business unit was set up and one of the metrics being tracked was the % of quotes accepted by customers. Higher is better with this metric. How can winning more jobs be counterproductive? One certain way is if jobs are underbid to the point where the company loses money on a regular basis. Is it a valid business strategy to quote a low price and work to reduce costs to the point of profitability? Certainly. However, underquoting price can be taken to an extreme to the detriment of the company.

The Quality department typically has authority for certain decisions including:
- Whether or not to ship product.
- Approving corrective actions/CAPAs.
- Determining whether a change requires customer notification or approval.
- Approving Document or Engineering Change Orders.
- Etc.

Using this authority to enable others to "go around" the system might make your job easier in the moment but will almost always make it more difficult in the long run. Many people will not view this as a one-off decision specific to a particular situation, rather they will turn it into an expectation for future decisions – that is, this will become the norm (see chapter 2, Normalization of Deviance). Why put this information in this chapter? Enabling people to go around the system encourages them to continue avoiding proper use of the system. **Obviously, any decision touching on ethics or compliance should not even be considered for authorizing a deviation.** This refers primarily to those "marginal" decisions where there is little or no risk or a procedure may be written in a manner that allows misinterpreting the intent. In such cases the practical side of your nature may argue that a specific task is not cost effective or necessary. Be forewarned however that your decisions will be scrutinized more than others for any sign of inconsistency.

It's often easier to provide incentive for the wrong behavior than for the intended behavior. Incentive systems that are not scrutinized for possible unintended consequences are actually more likely to provide incentive for wrong behaviors than for the intended ones. One must think carefully about how the incentive can be misinterpreted or twisted to serve an unintended purpose and then modify the incentive plan to minimize the chance that it will be, intentionally or unintentionally, distorted.

15 QE Relationship To Auditors and Inspectors

We live in a world consisting of shades of grey. Part of a Quality Engineer's job is to, as much as possible, turn that into a world of black and white for Quality Auditors and Inspectors. (note: the term "Auditors" in this chapter refers to people auditing product, not QMS auditors). This happens via creation of procedures, workmanship standards, etc. This is not to imply a lack of ability on the part of auditors or inspectors. Consider that the auditors and inspectors simply do not have the information to make some types of decisions independently. In addition to formal education, typically it is the Quality Engineers who are talking with the customer, in meetings with other engineers and management, conducting experiments to determine the effect of certain conditions on product performance (hence acceptability), analyzing data to ferret out information/meanings that are not apparent to a casual observer, attending seminars and other training, reading industry periodals, etc.

Imagine having to decide whether a product is conforming or nonconforming if the criteria is not clearly stated and the person needing to decide has never talked with the customer or hasn't seen the results of relevant engineering testing. That would be similar to someone else deciding which car to buy for you without knowing your preferences regarding price, features, color, etc.

Documenting procedures and criteria requires a skill that is often underestimated by the creators of those procedures/criteria. Examples follow.

Criteria: The part shall be yellow.
Ambiguity:
- What shade of yellow?
- Is it acceptable if a single part has two distinct shades of yellow?
- Is it acceptable if a single part has a consistent shade but is different than the part next to it?

74

- Which portion of the part needs to be yellow? The entire thing? If not, how much coverage is enough? At what point does a partial covering become nonconforming?
- What if one person thinks the part is "yellow enough" while the next person feels the opposite?
- How is the part to be inspected for color?
  - What type of lighting?
  - Where is the part located relative to the lighting?
  - Is magnification to be used?
  - Unaided eye? Corrected to 20/20?

Criteria with minimal ambiguity: The part shall be of uniform coloration, matching a designated visual sample, when inspected with unaided vision corrected to 20/20 and held at a distance of 12 – 18 inches from the eye under standard lab lighting as defined in specification INSP-0001.

Criteria: The computer program shall be user-friendly
Ambiguity:
- What does this mean?
  - Speed of execution?
  - Number of key strokes to accomplish a task?
  - Use of common vs. unfamiliar terms?
  - A stated reading level per a standard grading scale?
  - Doesn't crash very often?
    - What does "not very often" mean? A certain number of keystrokes or a unit of program run time? Other?
  - Other?

Criterial with minimal ambiguity:
  - A maximum of 3 keystrokes shall be required to access any primary software function as defined in SDD SOFT-0003.

Criteria: Track LED on-time
Ambiguity:
- Does this refer to the amount of time the device is powered on?

- Does this refer to the amount of time LEDs are being cycled (including the "off" portion of the cycle when they are not actively emitting light)?
- Does this refer to the amount of time the LEDs are actually emitting light?
- LED life estimates will vary greatly depending on which of the above is chosen. Interestingly, the estimates will all mean the same thing if one knows which criteria was used. I was involved in a project where all 3 definitions were assumed by various people on the project until we defined it more clearly.

Criteria with minimal ambiguity: Track the amount of time the LEDs are actively emitting light.

Criteria: No surface damage
Ambiguity:
- At what magnification?
  - Conditions not visible with the unaided eye can be readily seen under 10x magnification.
  - Conditions not visible under 10x magnification can be readily seen under 20x magnification.
  - All kinds of surface irregularities can be seen under an electron microscope.
  - Some conditions such as light reflections due to gradual bends are easier to see with the unaided eye than under magnification.
- Is discoloration considered surface damage?
- Is a scratch with no visible depth at 10x magnification considered surface damage?

Criteria with minimal ambiguity: No pits or scratches visible at 10x magnification.

People in QA/QC may take it personally when told they are not authorized to make certain decisions. It's important to explain this is not a knock on their abilities, rather a recognition that they don't have access to the information necessary to make those decisions.

Previous examples were Manufacturing related, but the concept easily extends to Service industries. Replace QE with Management and QA/QC Auditors/Inspectors with Customer Service, Barista, etc. and the following examples are appropriate.

Criteria: Provide friendly service
Ambiguity: what does this mean?
- Provide a smile to all customers?
- No customer waits more than 10 minutes?
- Greet customers?
- Use customer names?
- Go out on the floor at regular intervals to speak with customers?

Criteria with minimal ambiguity: Greet every customer with a smile, ask for their name, and address them by name for the duration of their visit. If the line appears as though any customer wait will exceed 5 minutes, call for additional staff from other areas of the establishment.

Criteria: provide fast service.
Ambiguity:
- What is fast? 30seconds? 2 minutes? 5 minutes? ½ hour? Every individual will have a personal definition and clearly "fast" is situation dependent.
  - A routine bank teller transaction rarely takes more than a few minutes.
  - A fast-food transaction should be over within a few minutes.
  - An oil change might be considered fast if complete in 10 minutes while a different car repair might be considered fast if it is complete within 24 hours.

Minimal ambiguity in this case is simple: define "fast" using a specific clock or calendar time – seconds, minutes, hours, days, weeks, etc.

16 How QE/RE add value to a company

I'm kind of weird even for an engineer in that I think statistics is fun. How does that statement relate to this chapter? Good Quality Engineers (QE) and Reliability Engineers (RE) bring a unique skill set to a company. In addition to being trained in engineering, design, and manufacturing principles, QEs and REs are often the resident experts in use of statistical methods in small and mid-size companies that can't afford dedicated statisticians. As a bonus, QEs and REs often have extra training in problem solving methods.

One way of adding value is to interpret standards and regulations and create methods that are compliant and work well for the business. Standards are written to apply to a broad range of companies and, as such, rarely apply exactly to any given company. They intentionally leave room for interpretation. Anyone with a high school education can read the standard and apply the strictest possible interpretation. However, this approach is often not the most useful for a given company. A QE should use his education, knowledge of the standard/regulation, and knowledge of the business processes to create systems and methods that are optimal for the company in which he is working at the time. This idea is covered more thoroughly in chapter 18.

The best QEs and REs in industry have a large toolbox, are adept at using many tools, and know when to choose the correct tool for a given situation. I want to be careful here. People who concentrate and become experts in a narrower toolset are vital in expanding the knowledge base for all to use! I refer to these experts as researchers. Small to medium businesses often cannot afford to pay researchers on staff. These people are often found in large companies, academia, and government. Again, a very valuable function different than the focus of this chapter. It's not uncommon for people to span the above descriptions. While most of my career has been spent as a QE/RE/Quality Manager, there have clearly been moments when I moved into the realm of researcher. Some of my most personally rewarding work, and some of the most valuable contributions to my employer, have been in this role. Example: I own a trade secret for a statistical model relating to performance of a finished product. Much of this was research-based, including consultations with a PhD statistician. It was one of the most rewarding projects in my career, but again the majority of my career has been spent as a practicing QE/RE/Manager in industry.

The large toolbox can be more important in Quality than other disciplines. In many companies, especially small to mid-size, a QE will interact with a wide range of the process and a wide range of other departments – suppliers, customers, regulators, Engineering, Sales, Purchasing, Manufacturing, etc. The QE will often lead problem-solving efforts or be used as a resource to help others lead these efforts.

Example 16.1: there are many RCA (Root Cause Analysis) and problem-solving tools. The 5-Why tool is appropriate in most situations – that is, it can add valuable insight across a wide range of problems. However, it is not always the best. Fishbone diagram is generally more powerful than 5-Whys and will view the problem from a broader perspective. FTA (Fault Tree Analysis) is even more powerful than fishbone diagram. On Time Delivery (OTD) is a many-faceted problem. It's affected by a wide range of departments/personnel, including Sales, Operations, Engineering, Quality, Materials, and even HR considering that staffing problems are often causes for missed ship dates. OTD includes personnel, ERP software considerations, machine downtime, process capability, and other considerations. 5-Whys would likely focus in only one area. If the problem is with a single late shipment, 5-Whys might provide the answer in the most efficient manner. If the problem is with low OTD across a range of products, customers, and manufacturing lines, 5-Whys will most likely be inadequate and either focus on a narrow aspect of the problem or be less efficient as the attempt is made to fit it to a problem where FTA would be more efficient. Why FTA over fishbone? A thorough OTD analysis covers multiple 11x17 pages in a FTA. One could cascade fishbones to address this issue, but FTA is even better suited. Another advantage of FTA is the ability to explicitly consider interactions among events through use of OR, AND, VOTING, and other gates. When considering OTD, using 5-Whys or fishbone diagrams feels painful to me compared to FTA. Conversely, 5-Whys is much more efficient than FTA when dealing with a narrower scope problem.

How many are aware of the synergistic relationship between FMEA (Failure Modes and Effects Analysis) and FTA? FMEA goes broad, considering every way a device, process, or system can fail. FTA goes deep, considering all of the causes and the interrelationship/interaction among those causes. I worked on a team designing a diagnostic medical device. We started with FMEA to consider all possible failure modes. When discussing an erroneous reading (wrong but believable?), we quickly realized the scope of the question and decided that FMEA was not adequate. We ended up with an 11-page FTA to list all potential causes of erroneous readings. To convey scope, I'll add that while most pages could be analyzed for minimal cut sets by a computer in 20 seconds or less, 1 of the 11 pages required the computer 5 minutes to analyze. The FTA contained hundreds of possible causes of failure. Most of those possible causes were so unlikely as to be considered to have a zero chance of failure. They were included for two reasons. First, presenting a complete FTA minimizes questions along the lines of "have you considered. . ." and delays associated with answering those questions. Second, a future design change might change the likelihood of any given cause manifesting. It was straightforward to assess the risk of each cause. The FMEA and FTA were created prior to product release, and drove us to multiple design changes that greatly improved the performance of the device when it was marketed.

Example 16.2: DOE (statistical Design Of Experiments) provides huge improvements in cost savings and effective results compared to traditional OFAT (One Factor At a Time) testing, yet these techniques are often electives if they are taught at all in colleges.

Knowledge of statistical methods is essential to avoid "wrong but believable" answers as discussed in chapter 5. Specific statistical methods are explored in other chapters, but this is not a book on statistics and barely scratches the surface regarding the benefits possible through proper analysis.

QEs/REs need to be fluent in a wide range of statistical analysis, design, and problem-solving tools. A very good, thorough overview of the types of tools can be found in the respective BOK (Body of Knowledge) required for certification by ASQ (American Society for Quality). Studying and sitting for these exams is a great way for a new QE/RE to gain exposure to the tools and quickly develop a level of competency in the discipline.

Maintain a corporate memory/history. Companies will sometimes cycle back and forth between competing ideas.

Example 16.3: A company had in place a cost-saving program that encouraged employees to submit and implement ideas. Some of the measurement equipment was expensive and difficult to operate so the (inexpensive) parts were brought to a central area to be measured and then scrapped. Since the measurements were nondestructive, someone suggested the scrap was too high and instead the parts be placed back into the manufacturing order after measurement so they could be sold to the customer. The idea was implemented. Shortly thereafter we received a customer complaint that they were sent someone else's parts (mixed parts). The cause was determined to be parts being returned to the wrong manufacturing order after measurement. The decision was made to scrap the parts after measurement (the original practice). Sometime later, a different person had the idea the scrap was too high and we should return the parts to the manufacturing order after measurement so they could be sold to the customer. The idea was again implemented until we received more customer complaints for mixed parts due to parts being returned to the wrong manufacturing order after measurement. This cycle was repeated at least one more time over the course of a few years. Each change required procedural updates and operator retraining and each of the customer complaints required investigation and corrective action. Considerable expense was invested each time a change was made, just to end up with the original procedure.

On a final note, it's important to understand that sometimes good ideas are ignored simply because the timing isn't right. The company may be inundated with other projects that are higher priority at the moment or the decision-maker at the time might not view the idea as particularly fruitful. **When you have a good idea that isn't immediately accepted, keep it handy to propose it again at a time when it is more likely to be approved and funded**.

17 Rewarding firefighting

If Management rewards firefighting at the expense of long-term improvement or preventive activities, it will create a company of firefighters who are also arsonists.

Consider: if employees are regularly rewarded for providing temporary, band-aid fixes to the problem of the day and, actively or through lack of recognition/reward, encouraged to avoid the long-term prevention of problems, the incentive is to at least let problems fester until the point where they raise to the level of a "fire" that warrants recognition/reward for putting out.

Does your company focus solely on daily meetings that deal with current problems or those that happened yesterday or does your company spend an equal amount of time on implementing permanent solutions to long term, chronic issues?

Does your company have a formal method for driving long-term improvements? Many methods can contribute to long-term improvements, including but not limited to:
- Formal management meetings where employees report on long term improvement activities.
- PLT (Product Line Teams) consisting of Engineering, Quality, Manufacturing that are held responsible for the long-term performance and improvement of a product line or product family.
- Formal improvement methods/programs.
  - Six Sigma/DMAIC (Define/Measure/Analyze/Improve/Control)
  - 8-D
  - PDSA (Plan/Do/Study/Act)
  - other
- Training programs that help people effectively use the improvement tools.
- CAPA (Corrective Action/Preventive Action)

- A method of quantifying or estimating financial and other benefits of long term improvement activities.

Quantifying the financial benefit of long-term improvements due to corrective actions is easier than those related to preventive actions. How do we know that a problem would have happened in absence of action to prevent it? If it would have happened, how can one determine how expensive it would have been? Rewarding prevention requires a management team that is committed to long term success, even when it may cause short-term expense, as well as one with the vision and commitment to persevere when the benefits are not immediately apparent.

Example 17.1: I worked on a medical device where we were encouraged to use the proper tools early in development to avoid failures later.
- A failure mode was identified through FMEA (Failure Modes and Effects Analysis).
- Testing confirmed that product would not meet requirements and would fail prematurely.
- The first attempt to fix the problem actually made it worse.
- The second attempted solution was successful.
- All of this activity occurred prior to the product launch.
- While we had ample evidence that the problem would have occurred on fielded units if not corrected, no lab test is perfectly representative of actual field use so we could not with high confidence quantify exactly how bad the issue would have been.
  - % failing units
  - Cost to replace failing units
  - Re-engineering a solution while in the midst of volume production
  - Upgrading susceptible, but not yet failed units
  - Residual costs including
    - Lost business
    - Liability risk

Of course, a company cannot chase every potential problem; doing so would result in a never-ending development cycle, a product that is never released to market, and a company that cannot remain in business. The trick is identifying those risks (potential problems) that will develop into hazardous or expensive problems if left unaddressed. Deciding where to assign a company's preventive resources can be a quite vexing problem due to the lack of quantifiable data for a problem that has not yet occurred. Tools such as Reliability Engineering, FMEA and FTA (Fault Tree Analysis), accelerated testing, and others exist for this type of assessment. A wise Management Team is forward-looking and focused on problem prevention.

Other metrics that can identify the need for preventive actions include:

- **NCR**. NCRs (NonConformance Report) can be very expensive. They result from a failure somewhere in the process. Typically, NCRs require investigation that is usually assigned to an Engineer who is already very busy with other activities. NCRs may be inevitable, but an excessive number points to a need for more preventive activities at the product or process design and development phase.
- **Scrap**. Scrap reduction typically goes straight to the bottom line and increases profits. And by the way, it improves quality going to the customer, especially when accomplished via activities to prevent the nonconforming product from ever being produced.
- **Customer complaints**.
- **Field failures**.
- **Litigation/liability.**

The reader might be thinking that the listed indicators are reactive when, by nature, preventive activities must be proactive. This is a true statement. However, one need only use the information provided by those indicators on current product and turn them into actions to prevent nonconformances on future products or processes.

18 Benefits of regulations and industry standards

Treating regulations and ISO/Industry standards as "a burden that must be put up with" is one of the larger mistakes that companies make.

Industry standards, such as ISO 13485, 14971 or 9001, and regulations such as 21CFR 820 often reflect good business practices. They are written in a general, rather than proscriptive, sense so they can be applied to a wide range of businesses. Understanding the business reasons behind the requirements makes for a much more effective QMS (Quality Management System) – one that provides net benefit and competitive advantage to a business - rather than one that creates a drag on the business. Quality professionals add value when they can see the business case behind the ISO requirements/FDA regulations and then apply them to their employer in a manner that helps the business.

Examples:

- Some companies don't see the value in proper document control practices, then don't get concerned when the wrong revision product is built for the customer and an entire job is scrapped. The link between document control and profits is not apparent, so they assign someone to write the procedure who doesn't understand the business reasons. This usually results in either a procedure with gaps, resulting in errors or a procedure that is inefficient because the person who wrote it interpreted the requirements incorrectly. Worst case, the procedure is both error-prone and inefficient.

- Training is often neglected. Proper training is required to ensure consistent methods and products. Inadequate training results in what Forrest Breyfogle calls the "hidden factory" – excessive costs due to scrap and inefficiencies that become accepted as "a cost of doing business". This hidden factory is a result of multiple different ways of performing a task, some of which are less efficient and produce a lower quality product. Hidden factory costs are insidious because they become part of the background noise

86

and often don't receive the focus to improve quality, reduce costs, and increase profits.

- ISO 13485 and 21CFR 820 require Standard Operating Procedures (SOPs) and Work Instructions (WIs). The business reason for these documents is to ensure consistent product to the customer and lower cost to the supplier by consistently using the most effective and efficient methods. Create SOPs and WIs that accomplish these objectives rather than creating SOPs and WIs "to comply with the standard". Lack of proper SOPs and WIs is almost certain to ensure that only some of the people do the right thing only some of the time.

Dealing with ISO and FDA requirements as a burden rather than good business can result in many problems, including:

- Inefficient business processes
- Resentment by employees who are expected to follow a process that they can clearly see is inefficient or wastes time
- Frustration by employees required to follow steps that they know are not efficient and that are not required by the standard or regulations
- Failure to follow procedures, resulting in field failures, liability problems, and audit findings
- Disagreement among departments with respect to what is actually required and the best way to meet those requirements
- Loss of credibility for the person who authored the procedure
- Procedures that fail to comply with regulations and/or industry standards.

Take ISO 14971 as an example. This is the recognized Risk Management standard for the medical device industry. The standard is written primarily for OEMs (Original Equipment Manufacturers or Legal Manufacturers). However, risk management is good business practice for a wide range of businesses. Consider a component manufacturer. They will not have the required information to comply with the entire standard, such as:

- Access to necessary design information to properly assess product risk. OEMs often are reluctant to share this detail.
- Access to field complaints. These go to the Legal Manufacturer, not a component manufacturer.
- Knowledge of the entire risk profile, including risk/benefit
- Detailed knowledge of product labeling.

Despite these knowledge gaps for component manufacturers, ISO 14971 contains much information useful to component manufacturers. Benefits to component manufacturers include:
- Risk management methods
  o Assessment
  o Evaluation
  o Control
- A component manufacturer is a better supplier if he/she understands the expectations placed on his/her customer and is fluent in the same (risk) language
- A proper risk management program as suggested in ISO 14971 will identify that actions such as exposing product to a new processing chemical, using a new material, or changing suppliers are high risk activities that should involve the customer early on. This reduces the risk of injury to users due to unapproved changes or upsetting customers by implementing an unapproved change or asking for short lead time on change approval.

Regular Management Review is a requirement in the Medical Device industry. The minimum expectation is to hold these reviews yearly with many companies preferring more a more frequent schedule. Management Review typically includes much of the senior management of a company or division. This is a very expensive meeting. A company that views standards/regulations as a necessary evil will have a meeting with pretty graphs that serve no useful purpose and waste the time of everyone in the meeting, not to mention those putting together the information. A company that recognizes the importance of Management Review will use it to make substantive decisions that improve the business.

Process validation is a requirement in the medical device industry. Many engineers and managers view validation as a burden and "just one more thing we have to do". However, as was recently made evident to me again, process validation allows us to identify and fix problems under controlled experimental conditions rather than dealing with failures during manufacturing. Manufacturing failures are often ill-defined and determining root cause can be challenging and time consuming. What is meant by ill-defined? Problems in manufacturing might not be reported for days, samples of the failures might not be available, important data might not be collected, etc. A properly run validation, in contrast, will collect information in a manner that greatly facilitates root cause analysis and problem solving.

Understanding the business reasons behind industry standards and regulations, and creating procedures that both comply with standards/regulations and are effective for the specific business, is one way for a Quality Department to add value to a business.

19 Internal competition

Internal competition can be good if managed properly. It can be a fun way to improve performance. Like any program, if mismanaged it can turn destructive.

Example 19.1: A 3 shift operation was set up so each shift was rewarded based on the number of parts produced on their crew. How did this turn destructive? Some crews would delay needed tooling maintenance and "let the next crew deal with it" who would in turn let the next crew deal with it, until the tooling simply stopped producing good product. This practice actually reduced, rather than improved, profit.

- Often nonconforming product was produced by the time the tool was sent for repair, requiring time be spent sorting or reworking the product.
- What would have been a ½ hour maintenance activity turned into a 6-hour repair.
- Sometimes tools that could have been maintained if taken out of service earlier were damaged beyond repair because of the need to "maximize output on my shift".
- Tool life was reduced via the practice of deferring maintenance until the tool reached a point where repair was required.
- Time was wasted trying to "tweak" other process parameters to compensate for a tool that was no longer performing properly.

In the same 3-shift operation, credit was given only for complete lots. Near the end of the shift, people would rush to complete the lot and get credit. It didn't matter to the employees if the lot failed the QC audit on the next shift because they already received credit and there was no mechanism for changing the numbers once credit was given.

How might one set up constructive competition in a situation like this? First, credit can only be given for "good" parts, including the results of QC inspection. Furthermore, customer feedback needs to be taken into account. If a lot is rejected by the customer, the metric for shift output needs to be adjusted accordingly. QC inspectors can be coerced into accepting product that should be rejected as is discussed elsewhere in this book. Second, a method must be in place to encourage tool maintenance while it is cost effective rather than allowing it to run until expensive repairs are required. Alternatively, competition may focus on other areas such as number of improvements or preventive actions implemented by shift.

Similar situations occur in many businesses – one simply needs to look for them.

20 Managing rapid growth

Rapid growth is something for which almost all businesses strive. It does, however, cause difficulties no matter how desirable. These difficulties include:

- Rapid growth means a lot of new people.
- New people make mistakes.
- Mistakes slow the process, reduce output, and increase customer complaints and returns.
- It takes time from experienced people to correct for the mistakes of the new people, further slowing the process.
- The faster the growth, the more severe the problems. Logically, these problems would grow at a faster than linear rate.

Tactics for managing rapid growth:

- Rock solid training system. Although not perfect, training is the most efficient, cost-effective way of preventing mistakes. A training system that works well during low-growth phases may not be adequate for rapid growth.
  - Training can only be effective with well-documented Work Instructions and/or training materials. This documentation will help ensure all trainers are saying, and all trainees are hearing, the same things.
    - The best that can be hoped for in the absence of good documentation is some of the people performing the task correctly some of the time.
  - Training adults is a skill in itself. Trainers need to be trained in this skill. The best operator may not be the best trainer.
  - Trainers have an outsized impact on performance as their habits and attitudes not only affect their work, but are conveyed in the training and likely affect the work of the trainees when they are on the job.

- Over-staff in the short term to provide the resources to deal with the additional time requirements created by the large influx of new people.
  - This requires a leap of faith by management that the growth is real and sustainable. When growth tapers, the "extra" staff are absorbed into the workforce in place of additional hires.
    - Short-term cost targets can provide difficulty gaining approval for this strategy.
  - Remember from above that new employees create mistakes that need to be corrected by the experienced employees. This takes time, resulting in fewer parts. Reduced output results in higher pressure which further increases mistakes, requiring more time to correct and further reducing output. Over time and as the new people gain experience, these problems will minimize – assuming the company survives long enough. Only Management can prevent this wasteful cycle by properly planning for the growth and taking positive action to minimize the negative impact.
- While training is essential, no training program can completely substitute for experience. As such, it is important to consciously arrange for more experienced employees to be available as a reference for the newly trained employees. Having experienced employees at hand to answer questions raised by the new employees goes a long way toward maintaining efficiency during a time of rapid growth.
- The previous suggestions work synergistically. Either alone is less effective than when paired with the other.
- Can a company grow successfully without adoption of these principles? Of course, it can. The more relevant question is "How do we best serve our customers, maintain efficiency, and maximize profit during the period of rapid growth?" This latter question requires that we recognize the inherent challenges posed by rapid growth and plan to address them directly.

- I was fortunate enough to be in position as a department manager for a new manufacturing site that was being built and successfully used the listed tactics.
  - Our department caused fewer processing delays, made correct decisions at a higher rate, and was more efficient than departments that did not focus on these factors.

21 Which is more important, efficiency or effectiveness?

I was asked this question in an interview years ago and gave the wrong answer. At the time, I made the case that the answer was situation-specific. After considerable deliberation, it became clear to me that, while both are important, effectiveness is the more important.

Part of the definition of effectiveness at Dictionary.com is "producing the intended or expected result". Something that is not effective then is not producing the intended result. What benefit is provided by efficiently performing a task that does not accomplish anything useful? In other words, **it is not beneficial to do quickly something that should not be done at all or that leads to a wrong answer/decision.**

The rotary dial phone example might help illustrate. We might be the most efficient at making rotary dial phones, but if nobody wants to buy one, our business will not be very successful.

RCA (Root Cause Analysis) is required to prevent problems from recurring. Finding an answer quickly is efficient and desirable, but only if it's the right one. Rushing to the wrong answer may seem like we've done something useful, but if it didn't solve a problem it was a complete waste of time. Worse, if it led to the wrong action we may have made the problem worse or created new problems. "Wasting time efficiently" is an oxymoron.

As another example, FMEA activities are often erroneously performed by a single Engineer at her/his desk, maybe in less than an hour, to check it off the list as completed. A cross-functional team is typically required to create a truly effective FMEA. Consider two scenarios:

1. A cross-functional team of 4 Engineers spends 20 hours in team meetings, resulting in a FMEA that saves millions of dollars in preventable product failures/returns.

95

2. A single Engineer fills out the FMEA form in 30 minutes, but fails to identify the preventable failures, resulting in millions of dollars in returns that needn't have occurred.

In the second scenario, the FMEA form was completed at less than 1/100 of the cost **but did not provide any useful function**. Clearly, the second scenario was more efficient if one measures efficiency only in time spent to perform a task, yet cost millions of dollars more by failing to provide the intended result (failing to be effective).

96

22 Important, Urgent, Both, or Neither?

Throughout my career, I've seen many people get caught up in firefighting and unable to break out of that mode. A task can be categorized multiple ways. A categorization scheme that has been effective is to list the task as important, urgent, both, or neither. This is illustrated in the matrix below.

		Important?	
		No	**Yes**
Urgent?	**Yes**	Distraction **2**	Crisis Management **1**
	No	Waste of time **3**	Most effective use of time **4**

Figure 5 – Important/Urgent Matrix

Let's define the terms. Important means completion of the task will have a significant effect on business success. Urgent means there is a driver to complete the task quickly or in a short time.

Do you feel obligated to open every e-mail the moment it arrives in the inbox? Are you constantly interrupted by the phone or by people walking into your cubicle or office? All of us have to learn how to prioritize workload and deal with the daily demands. Let's examine the 4 quadrants of the matrix to explore this further.

Quadrant 1 – important and urgent. Issues in this quadrant need to be addressed quickly. Examples would include: equipment that is down and needed for production, an irate customer on the phone, an injury or illness at work, your boss is demanding the task be done immediately, etc. Many people think this quadrant is where their time is spent most effectively. The combination of important and urgent often, but not always, places these tasks in the category of crisis management or firefighting. The urgent component of the task will often result in a temporary or short-term solution, sometimes referred to as a band-aid. This type of solution fixes the immediate problem, but in such a manner that it is likely to recur.

Quadrants 2 and 3 are similar and will be addressed together – urgent, but not important or neither urgent nor important. These issues are at best distractions and at worst a waste of time. They may demand your time in the moment, but don't contribute very much or at all to the success or failure of the business and should be avoided when possible. This is **not** an excuse to be intentionally rude or uncaring. It's a realization that certain events need to be managed so that our time on the job may be used to the best advantage. Examples would include:

- Unnecessary e-mails. How many of us have been the recipient of "reply to all" that consist primarily of (seemingly) endless acknowledgements or thank you messages intended for a single recipient? Acknowledging and showing gratitude to others is vital to good working relationships, but can be taken to extremes, especially when reply to all is in the mix.
- Telemarketing phone calls for services or products in which you have no interest.
- Paperwork coming across your desk, requiring attention, but serving no useful purpose.

Issues in these quadrants are best ignored when possible. E-mails can be deleted without being opened, although this does risk missing some unexpected content and needs to be done with care. Phone calls can be screened. Unnecessary paperwork can be eliminated.

Quadrant 4 – important, but not urgent. This quadrant is often where the most effective use of time is found. It's here where permanent solutions to problems are often identified and implemented or, better yet, where problems are prevented. Most people understand the problems with quadrants 2 and 3 although some are not very effective at handling them, but the difference between quadrants 1 and 4 is not obvious to many. Examples may better illustrate.

- If a machine is down, getting it running again is a quadrant 1 activity. Preventing future breakdowns is a quadrant 4 activity.
- In case of an injury, first-aid is a quadrant 1 activity. Preventing future injuries is a quadrant 4 activity.
- In CAPA terms, "correction" is often a quadrant 1 activity and "corrective action" quadrant 4.
- If a procedure is found to be wrong, issuing a waiver or deviation would be a quadrant 1 activity and permanently changing the procedure would be quadrant 4.

I've been known at more than one employer to ignore interruptions or to "hide out" when necessary to work in quadrant 4. Hiding out often consists of finding an unused conference room from which to work or working in the cafeteria where people are less likely to find me. While we can be made to feel that every e-mail or phone call must be responded to immediately, I have not been fired or reprimanded for working in quadrant 4 – to the contrary, I have often been commended for being productive. Consciously deciding to spend time in quadrant 4 has much to do with both individual and business success. As with other techniques suggested in this book, one needs to be prudent in applying this one. Some managers may be less tolerant of this particular tactic than others. While my managers have focused on results and have chosen to support, or at least not reprimand, the "hiding out to focus on quadrant 4 work" tactic, others might not see the benefit or might not be open to that particular tactic for completing one's task list. Remember that certain quadrant 1 activities are important enough that we need to drop everything to address them immediately. The tactic of hiding out or ignoring distractions is typically restricted to 2-8 hour blocks of time. In the rare instances where larger blocks of time are required, it's prudent to make sure your manager knows and approves of the tactic in advance. One key point if you are going to use this tactic – **you need to show results** (scary, isn't it?).

23 Any process can be flow charted

Corollary: If a process is not flow charted, its efficiency cannot be proven.

Flow charts, despite being around for decades and despite the promotion of Value Stream Mapping, swim lane charts, and related methods, are still under-utilized in many companies. I've even heard comments along the lines of "this process can't be flow charted, it's more of an art". Don't believe it. Any process can be flow charted. Furthermore, a process cannot be proven efficient or completely effective unless and until it is flow charted. Flow charting can be used across a wide range of problems - order processing, manufacturing, office procedures, Document Control methods, Risk Management, essentially any series of actions that accepts inputs and changes them into outputs. As a general rule, the most successful people I've seen use flow charts effectively. Those who avoid flow charts are typically less effective at their job.

The benefit examples are so numerous that it is difficult to choose only a few. Many of the details are proprietary, but not necessary to illustrate the benefits:

- A company was having difficulty with extended process development cycles. Everyone knew there was waste in the system, but no two people would describe either the process or waste the same way. Involvement from many people was required to create the "current flow". When documented and agreed upon as accurate, Management was shocked at the waste in the system.
  - o Steps that should take a week or two could take 4 months
  - o Document review/approval was done serially – documents would sit on one person's desk for a day to many days, be processed, then go to the next desk to sit for a day or more, etc. – there were many more than two desks on which to languish.
  - o The process was subjected to unnecessary review steps causing more delay.

- o Literally months of delays could be easily taken out of the process with a little planning, yet these delays had been tolerated for years.
- A complaint/CAPA system for a medical device company needed to be improved. The system was described in a procedure, but had never been flow charted. The system as described wasn't working since it was identified as an audit finding, hence the need for improvement.
  - o The current process was charted and the gap leading to the finding easily identified.
  - o A new process was created to close the gap and make other improvements.
  - o The new, improved process unfortunately created new gaps that needed to be closed. Why is this included here? The new process was flow charted prior to implementation. The flow chart is the only reason the gaps were identified and corrected **before** causing a problem.
- Benefits of flow charting include
  - o Elimination of unnecessary steps
  - o Elimination of "dead end" or incomplete paths. These are particularly troublesome situations in that they can lead to a process that produces incomplete, sporadic, erroneous, or even dangerous results. This is key to improving effectiveness.
  - o Elimination of unnecessary delays
  - o Elimination of unnecessary costs
  - o Improved efficiency
  - o Minimizing errors
  - o Improve communication/understanding. I've seen written procedures where college-educated engineers could not agree on the proper order of steps or meaning of some of the instructions. A flow chart not only created agreement among the engineers, but eased communication to the operators who had to follow the procedure.

The concept of flow charting is easy. Record the required actions and decisions in the order they are supposed to occur. Connect with lines/arrows to demonstrate the paths to follow. Look for duplicated or unnecessary steps, missing steps, error-prone steps, and modify the process to improve it. The practice of creating flow charts, however, can be frustrating. Often a team is required because the process will span multiple departments or multiple processes and no one individual knows every detail. People will be convinced that different methods or steps are required or that the steps should be in a different order. Leading the team can be more challenging than the act of charting the process on paper!

So why do some people still not utilize flow charts when doing so would improve their effectiveness? I'm not sure of the answer, but a few possibilities come to mind.

1. Don't know how. Flow charting is an easy concept and easy to train, so this reason should not prove problematic.
2. Not convinced of the benefits. This can often be corrected by selecting an intractable or annoying problem and illustrating the benefits of using a flow chart to solve/improve. Not all people are convinced by this. When needed, as a manager I will simply require a flow chart before reviewing/approving a SOP, Work Instruction, or other document. This doesn't always make friends, but almost always results in a better document.
3. Perceive the benefits, but think the time to create a control chart is prohibitive. On a related note, some may perceive the benefits but believe they can achieve the same results without going through the effort of creating a flow chart. This is the most common situation in which I will sometimes need to require a flow chart prior to reviewing/approving a document.
4. Lazy. This is said tongue-in-cheek but is a valid consideration. Maybe we choose to use a different word for it, but there is often a temptation to take the shortest, easiest path even when it is not the most effective path.

Two simple flow charts are demonstrated in figure 6 for any who might not be familiar with the term. If we consider that every approval process can take from 1 hour to 1 week, the top process may take anywhere from 4 hours to 4 weeks while the bottom will always be completed within a single week. If using a paper-based system, the parallel approval process can be achieved by sending an electronic copy for review and maintaining the copy to be signed in a central location.

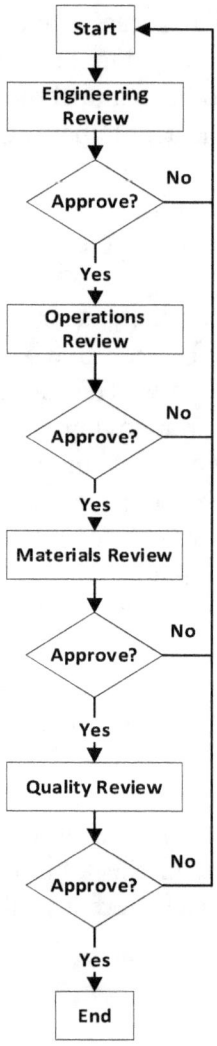

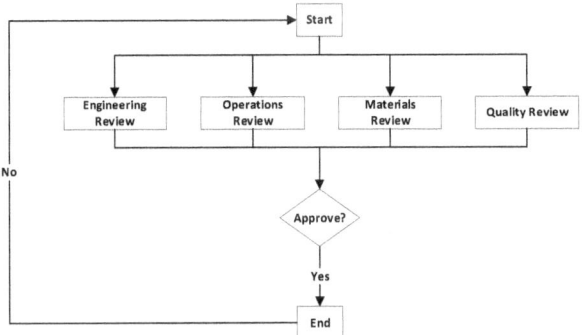

Figure 6 – Flow Charts

A second benefit is obvious from the flow charts. In the serial process, we might have waited more than 3 weeks before Quality disapproves the document and repeating the process might add another 4 weeks. In the parallel flow, any disapproval from any department is obtained within a week and repeating the process is completed within a second week. In addition, in the parallel flow feedback can be obtained from all reviewers concurrently. In contrast, in the serial flow it is common for one or more reviewers to approve only to have someone further down the line disapprove. This cycle can repeat multiple times.

24 Myth: Correlation = causation

Reality: Correlation can occur from a coincidence of timing. Causality is a much stronger relationship.

Examples (note: some of these examples were found via internet search and were taken at face value – these are identified):

- Implementation of a new chamfer tool coincided with elimination of burrs. Chamfer tool did not eliminate burrs, rather other tooling changes implemented at the same time fixed the problem.
- Divorce rate in Maine from 2000 to 2009 is correlated to the per capita consumption of margarine (internet). Does eating margarine lead to divorce?
- Age of Miss America from 1999 to 2009 was correlated to the number of murders by steam, hot vapor and hot objects. (internet)
- Marriage rate in Kentucky from 1999 to 2010 was correlated with the number of people who drowned after falling out of a fishing boat. (internet)
- Rates of violent crime increase along with sales of ice cream. Does committing a violent crime cause a craving for ice cream? Does eating ice cream make one violent?
  - This one could be an example of a third factor causing both of the items observed to be correlated. I live in Minnesota. People both spend more time outside at night and buy more ice cream in summer when the weather is nice. It is logical that warm weather would drive more ice cream sales and lead to more people hanging out on the streets late at night. It is also logical that the more often large crowds congregate late at night the higher the likelihood for crime. Neither ice cream nor hanging around outside are very desirable at 20 degrees below zero.
- Airplane ride gets bumpy when seat belt light is turned on. Does the seatbelt light cause turbulence?

- o This one does include a causal relationship in the reverse order. Turbulence cause both the plane ride to get bumpy and the pilot to turn on the seatbelt light.
- PAD (Peripheral Artery Disease) is correlated with heart attack risk. Does PAD cause heart attacks? Do heart attacks cause PAD? Multiple headlines/advertisements seem to imply that PAD causes heart attacks. They don't directly state so, but make the implication based on the correlation.
  - o In reality, both are caused, at least in part, by plaque build-up in arteries.
- I offer training and consulting in quality and reliability tools. When I promote those tools, it's natural for people to assume I'm promoting them to drum up business for myself. While of course this is partially true, the assumption mixes up cause and effect. I don't promote the tools because I'm in the business, rather I'm in the business first and foremost because I believe in the effectiveness of the tools/methods. While promoting tools for which I offer training/consulting will have the effect of drumming up business, it's not the primary reason for the promotion. This might seem like a fine distinction to some, but to me it's key. I'm not a good salesman and have never been able to effectively promote ideas in which I don't believe. I considered trying to develop that "talent" (promoting something in which I don't believe) but decided it's not who I want to be.

25 Myth: MTBF is the best reliability metric for me

Reality: MTBF **may** be the best metric, but only if certain conditions are met. MTBF is certainly the metric most often used inappropriately.

This myth has been debunked repeatedly and by many authors, but the mistake still occurs on a regular basis.

MTBF stands for Mean Time Between Failure. MTBF, as commonly used, assumes an exponential distribution. Also implied is a repairable system since we are discussing time between failure (implying multiple failures).

The exponential distribution:
- Exhibits a constant failure rate and is memoryless
    - The chance that the device will fail today is the same chance that it will fail this date next year or the chance it will fail on April 12, 2025 or the chance that it will fail August 27, 2031 (for example).
    - An exponential distribution implies that testing 1000 devices for 1000 hours each is equivalent to testing 1 device for 1,000,000 hours. Is it reasonable to claim 1,000,000-mile MTBF for car tires if 1000 tires each survive for 1000 miles? Of course not, but it's the implication when we use the MTBF metric (this ignores for the moment the non-repairable nature of worn out tires).
- Is easy to integrate, making the math more tractable.
- Is not appropriate if a device is expected to wear out (increasing failure rate).
- Does not apply to infant mortality situations (decreasing failure rate).
- Implies a repairable system.

When does the exponential distribution apply? Many electronic components exhibit an approximately constant failure rate during much of their useful life. Imagine a television with a 20-year design life. A circuit board inside that television may have a design life of 150 years. During the 20-year TV design life, the circuit board may follow an approximately exponential distribution. Also, Drenick's theorem states that reliability of complex systems approaches an exponential distribution as the number of components and time of operation increase, regardless of the underlying reliability distribution of individual components. Assumptions/constraints to the theorem include:

- Components are in series
- Components fail independently
- Failed components are immediately replaced
- Identical replacement components are used

What to do when the exponential distribution does not apply? Determine the proper distribution (Weibull, lognormal, etc.) and calculate MTTF (Mean Time To Failure) or MTTFF (Mean Time To First Failure) rather than MTBF. Detailed discussion of reliability analysis methods such as these are a topic for a different time.

26 Set Your Own Course ("To Thine Own Self Be True" – William Shakespeare)

Every Quality professional I know who has been in a decision-making role for any reasonable length of time has been asked to do something unethical and the ethical line may not always be obvious. The previous statement is based in part on my experience and in part on conversations with other Quality/Reliability professionals. The request can come from peers, subordinates, supervisors, customers, suppliers – almost anyone. I did not include this chapter in the first edition of the book out of concern that readers might **incorrectly** attribute the issues listed here to my current or past supervisors. None of the specific examples here occurred at my current employer unless otherwise stated.

It would be easy to misinterpret this chapter as casting aspersions on some very honorable people to whom I have reported, so I want to be very clear. **I have never left a job/company over ethical concerns. When I had to take an ethical stand, my managers have been very supportive. I consider myself lucky in this regard.** The vast majority of requests for unethical behavior came from other sources, some of which are mentioned above. I'm particularly sensitive that this chapter is not interpreted to reflect upon any particular person or company. The interested reader need only watch the newspapers/internet news feeds to pursue this subject further. Chapter 2 contains some specific examples of unethical corporate behaviors.

The American Society for Quality (ASQ) has a code of ethics with which members are expected to comply. It would be nice to live in a world where ethical behavior is a given and might seem kind of silly to require a documented code. It doesn't take much time reviewing news stories to understand that we do not live in such a world. As illustrated below, I have run into ethical quandaries in my job and the Quality professional should prepare herself/himself for just such an eventuality.

Over my career I have been asked to:
- Back date my signature on documents

- Falsify data
- Knowingly approve shipment of nonconforming product
- Ignore sampling results and re-sample the lot until it passed
- Re-measure a part until the measurement was acceptable
- Make a decision that would result in short-term financial gain for me at the long-term expense of the company
- A customer asked us to claim good parts as having "no value" to avoid paying a fee at Customs
- Lie to a customer "because Sales lied to the customer"
- Share proprietary information with people who did not have a right or need to know
- Withhold information that was necessary to share

A few of these requests are of particular note and specific examples are expanded upon below.

Example 26.1:
Very early in my career, approximately 30 years ago, an experiment being run for a customer was messed up. I don't remember if I had a hand in messing it up, but I clearly remember my manager at the time instructing me to make up results different than what we obtained and consistent with what we expected the experiment to yield – in other words to falsify data. **This is the only time I remember being asked by a direct supervisor/manager to perform unethically.** I am still ashamed to admit that I followed the instructions and reported false data. At the time my wife, young son, and I were living paycheck to paycheck. I remember thinking I could not risk losing my job. Even so, the issue bothered me nonstop for days until I decided that no job was worth my integrity. I told the manager to never ask me to do something like that again and, despite my fears, I did not get fired for insubordination. Interestingly, that manager and I had a very good relationship for many years after this event. For the record, the particular experiment was not very significant in the scheme of things and the industry was not regulated; still the behavior was clearly unethical. To this day I do not know why the request was made and can only surmise that it would have been embarrassing to admit the mistake or the company didn't want to invest the resources in repeating the experiment.

Example 26.2:
A few years after that, I was having a discussion with someone from Customer Service (CS) regarding an issue. I remember telling her that I could not make a certain statement because it was not true and I would not lie to a customer. She promptly proceeded to tell me that "if Sales lies to a customer, you will lie to the customer". I disagreed on the spot and terminated the conversation. I was quite livid and went to find my manager. Based on previous experiences, I was ready to resign immediately if my manager agreed with the CS Representative. Fortunately, he told me to chill, of course he did not expect me to lie to a customer, and he'd take care of the issue. I never heard any more about it and apparently he took care of it – nobody in Sales ever asked me to lie to a customer again.

Example 26.3:
An Engineering Manager one day asked me to come to the cafeteria for a discussion. I was Quality Manager at the time. We both had offices so I'm not sure why he chose the cafeteria, maybe because it seemed a more relaxed setting. He was proposing that I approve a course of action which I deemed to not be in the best long-term interest of our employer. I remember his words "there's a pile of money out there and we should grab our share". He was referring to the bonus program in place by our employer. I don't remember the particulars of his proposal, but remember clearly my impression – the action was likely to increase profits short term and, yes, would likely increase our yearly bonus as a result, but was also likely to place in jeopardy the long-term health/viability of our employer. I declined to approve the proposed course of action. Probably the worst result of that particular interaction is the loss of trust and respect for the Engineering Manager. We continued to work together, but I had a hard time trusting him and taking his proposals at face value henceforth.

Example 26.4:
The unethical behaviors mentioned in this chapter can have other unintended consequences. This example did occur at my current employer. The unethical request came from a customer who requested that we mark parts as "no value" to avoid paying a fee at customs. A Salesperson at my employer was leading the call and when the request arose, so I decided to stay quiet and see how it played

112

out, knowing that I could always intervene later if we failed to do the right thing. To his credit, the Salesperson immediately replied along the lines of "We can't do that". Despite our Salesperson doing the right thing, a young engineer who was on the call came to me and stated that "he didn't even want to work on that customer's product any more, in fact he wanted nothing to do with that customer or their products". The single customer request completely disincentivized the engineer to work on their product. The loss of trust inherent in promoting wrong behaviors will last much longer than the initiating event. The particular customer was a startup company that eventually went out of business.

The reader might be wondering about the purpose of this chapter. It's definitely not to embarrass or cast aspersions on any individual or company. I was naïve and surprised by some of the things that were asked of me. For anyone new to the Quality profession, I would suggest you spend some time thinking about this issue, defining your set of principles, and deciding where to draw your personal line with respect to ethics. Let's be clear, it's not always apparent when something crosses the line between ethical and unethical and people can legitimately have differing opinions regarding the location of that line. That's why it's important to consider the issue in advance and think about how we might respond to certain situations. Of course, it's impossible to predict exactly what will be asked of us or how we might react in a specific situation, but it's much easier to respond to a variety of situations having considered in advance some of the possibilities. As Shakespeare wrote in Hamlet, "to thine own self be true".

There are definite shades of grey when it comes to what is ethical. Let's look at some of the previous examples from a different perspective to illustrate this point.

Falsifying data is and always will be unethical. How can the line be blurred in this type of situation? What if we have an outlier? An outlier here would be defined as a measurement that we know to be in error and not representative of the true results. In this situation, it is proper and ethical to exclude the outlier from the analysis. How then should one document this? Can we just ignore the outlier and leave it out of the report? (The answer to this question is an emphatic no). If not, how is the outlier documented? Is it included in the report along with an explanation regarding why it is an outlier and excluded from the analysis (this is my personal preference)? In an appendix? Separate from the report but in a referenced document? Separate from the report, in a document not directly referenced in the report? In a separate report? Buried in someone's desk knowing we can find it if we need it? Somewhere in here is the line between ethical and unethical and there can be legitimate difference of opinion regarding the exact location of that line.

Lying to a customer is and always will be unethical. What if instead the CS Rep had asked me to withhold information from the customer? If the customer had requested the information and it was directly relevant to their product, withholding would have been unethical. What if the information was relevant to the customer but of no real importance? What if the CS Rep knew, based on previous conversations, that the customer really wasn't interested in the information and it would only add confusion to an already confusing situation? What if the customer had requested proprietary information from a different customer? In this last case, it would be unethical to share, rather than withhold, the information requested by the customer. Again, nuances can make the ethical/unethical line unclear and different people can legitimately differ on the exact location of that line.

Using one's position for her/his own benefit at the expense of one's employer is and always will be unethical. What if the short-term benefit is certain, but the long-term impact not certain? Clearly profit, whether short or long-term, is the goal of any commercial business. Assuming the short-term profit is easy to predict, when does the decision become an ethical concern? What if there is 10% chance the long-term impact will be neutral or even positive? 30%? 50%? 70%? 90%? All business decisions have some uncertainty regarding outcome. In this scenario, if one expects a reasonable likelihood that the long-term impact will be positive, approving the proposal is ethical. The question becomes "what is reasonable likelihood?". Again, differing opinions on the exact location of the ethical line can be legitimately held.

Before anyone thinks this issue is specific to an industry or a company, I would suggest you pick up the newspaper, a news magazine, or simply browse the internet for a while. News stories involving unethical, even illegal, behavior occur almost nonstop – insider trading, embezzlement, hiding or manipulating

114

test results related to consumer health, suppressing information related to field failures/hazards, cheating on taxes, lawmakers pushing legislation to benefit themselves, etc., etc., etc.

My wife (Kari) worked for a nonprofit organization. As with many nonprofits, they would conduct drives for donations and encourage the employees to donate. While they were very careful to state that donations were voluntary, they would make statements along the lines of "we appreciate everyone's support because now we can tell our donors that all staff participate". Although the business was careful to state that the donations were voluntary, the peer pressure and guilt were such that it did not **feel** voluntary. Nobody wanted to be the only person who didn't participate and thereby deprive the business of the ability to "tell donors that all staff participate".

Questions like this often fall into one of seven categories:
- "This is a best practice". If it's good for the company, it's an easy decision.
- "I can support that practice". While maybe not best practice, there are no ethical concerns.
- "I can live with that". Again, no ethical concerns, but this one requires a little more thought.
- "It makes me uncomfortable". This one requires the most thought since it's clearly approaching that line and likely in the grey area where there can be legitimate disagreement regarding the ethical course of action.
- "That appears unethical". This and the previous category represent the most difficult situations. You may feel obligated to take a stand yet honest differences of opinion may exist.
- "That's clearly unethical". This one is easy if we have a firm foundation in principles as explained in chapter 2.
- "That's illegal". This one again is relatively easy since it's based on facts rather than on opinion.

I would be doing the reader a disservice if I excluded the cautions. A person may not always be rewarded for doing the right thing. I remember a Marketing Manager who disagreed with the company line regarding future orders/revenue. The company line was to believe orders/revenue would continue along a steep growth trajectory. I was in the meeting where this particular Marketing Manager laid out the case that the data did not match the forecast and he did not believe we would maintain the growth trajectory. It's important to note he was the only person who was right, or told the truth, maybe both. Despite being right and telling the truth, when the next layoff happened a short time later, this person was let go. Was it because he was the only one in Marketing who told the unpleasant truth? Were there other issues that caused him to be let go? Was he treating others poorly (knowing him, I seriously doubt this)? I can't be certain. The timing, however, was suspicious. See chapter 24 regarding why correlation does not equal causation for more explanation why timing alone does not allow us to draw the conclusion the action resulted in the layoff.

I was in a meeting with a different company where a long-term regulatory consultant spoke what the rest of us were thinking. In the meeting, management clearly did not like the message and his contract was not renewed. Again, were there other factors at play that caused the contract to not be renewed? The timing causes one to be suspicious, but correlation does not equal causation and admittedly I don't have enough information to draw a firm conclusion.

Despite these cautions, I've found often that increased respect and credibility is the result of taking a proper ethical stand.

27 Use of r^2 for measurement correlation is misleading

Linear regression seems a natural method to compare two measurement systems. After all, regression quantifies the correlation between two phenomena, in this case measurements made by a supplier and measurements on the same parts made by a customer. When regression is used in this manner, r^2 is the common metric used to determine whether two measurement systems are adequately correlated. r^2 is called the coefficient of determination. More information on this statistic can be found in [Devore, p. 465]. Use of regression in this fashion, however, can be quite misleading.

I first ran into the problem decades ago while working for a company selling products to a large corporation. The customer required that r^2 between their measurement system and that of the supplier exceed 0.8. The correlation studies exhibited r^2 much less than 0.8 and the measurement systems were rejected by the customer. This was odd since the process Cpk was on the order of 12, providing the first clue that the problem was not related to measurement capability or correlation, rather a lack of variability in the product.

After much discussion, the customer's statistics department agreed that the test samples for such a correlation study should cover the entire range of the tolerance. The tolerance in this case was +/- 0.002 inch. The product was made using a sheet metal forming process. **Creating parts to cover the tolerance range would have required us to grind a tool that was making almost perfect parts and force it to make marginal parts, with no assurance we could return the tool to its original state**. This would need to be done twice to manufacture parts near both the upper and lower tolerance limits. Readers can imagine the response if someone were to ask a Toolmaker to take a perfectly good tool, grind it to make marginally high parts, then grind it to make marginally low parts, then return it to pristine state – all for the purpose of performing a measurement correlation study. If you've worked with Toolmakers before, you're likely

117

cringing right now. They are not known for putting up with nonsense and needless to say, this discussion would not have gone well and was not attempted.

To make a long story short, the statistician at the customer suggested we place a guard band around the tolerance to ensure that measurement correlation never resulted in nonconforming product. The tolerance was +/- 0.002 inch, the Cpk on the order of 12, and the suggested guard band 0.000050 inch. The resulting "effective tolerance" was +/- 0.00195 inch. While philosophically regression was the wrong tool to apply, from a practical standpoint it was easy to agree to the guard band, confident in the knowledge that it would never cause us as the supplier to take action. Figure 27.1 illustrates the situation and clearly shows that the guard bands had no practical impact on the business.

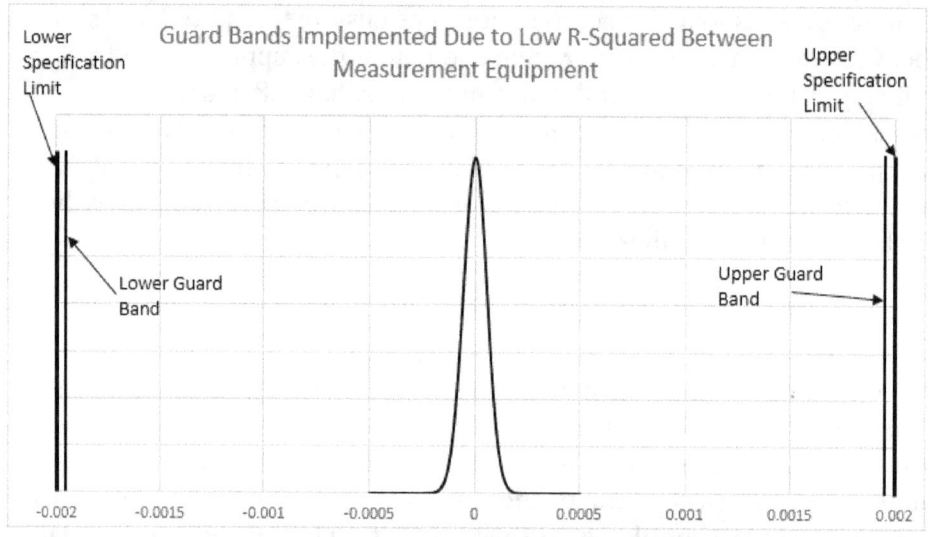

Figure 27.1 – Measurement Guard Bands

[Nachtsheim] illustrates in detail why use of regression to compare measurement systems is often misleading. A simple example is included here for illustration. Sample data is different from the data used in

Nachtsheim, but the methods are analogous and lead to the same conclusions.

Assume:
- Regression analysis is used for a correlation study with 25 pieces.
- The measured value is made up of some true value plus random measurement error from either the customer or supplier as appropriate.
  - Note: the true value is never known since there is no way to determine it other than by measuring and every measurement has some error associated with it.
    - Some measuring gages have error low enough that we may accept the measured value as truth. Think of NIST provided values, although even these are provided with an uncertainty statement.

Scenario 1:
- True values are modeled as iid N(50, 5)
  - iid stands for independent and identically distributed
  - N(50,5) refers to a normal distribution with mean 50 and standard deviation 5
  - This is done in practice by generating 25 random numbers in Excel or a statistical analysis package from a normal distribution with mean of 50 and standard deviation of 5.
- Customer measurement error is modeled as iid N(0, 5)
- Supplier measurement error is modeled as iid N(0, 5)

What does this mean? The customer and supplier measurement systems are identical. Neither is biased with a mean error of zero and they have the same amount of random measurement error as indicated by the common standard deviation of 5. Parts will measure different at the customer compared to the supplier only because of the random measurement error at the time of measurement.

Measured value for each of the 25 parts at the customer is then modeled as true value plus random measurement error and analogously for measured values at the supplier.

$$m_{c,i} = t_i + e_{c,i}$$
$$m_{s,i} = t_i + e_{s,i}$$

In the above equations:
- m refers to the measured value
- subscript c refers to the customer
- subscript s refers to the supplier
- subscript i refers to the ith part
- t refers to the true (unknown) value
- e refers to random measurement error

Table 27.1 contains the values for this simulation and figure 27.2 the resulting regression analysis.

True Value	Customer Measurement Error	Supplier Measurement Error	Customer Measured Value	Supplier Measured Value
44.997	-0.747	7.145	44.250	52.142
57.627	-6.928	-3.809	50.699	53.818
45.973	-5.913	-0.366	40.060	45.607
48.003	4.981	-2.274	52.983	45.729
46.414	9.819	0.839	56.233	47.253
52.397	-6.293	-3.633	46.104	48.764
49.298	-6.807	6.336	42.491	55.634
57.767	0.891	-6.658	58.658	51.109
48.414	4.904	-1.384	53.318	47.03
41.860	2.934	-4.930	44.794	36.93
47.640	4.390	2.063	52.030	49.703
48.677	-6.012	-7.084	42.665	41.593
53.260	2.351	-0.454	55.611	52.806
54.848	1.624	-3.440	56.472	51.408
42.093	1.604	1.187	43.697	43.28
52.872	-0.970	-7.733	51.902	45.139
54.114	-2.717	-6.741	51.397	47.373
53.342	7.412	-6.388	60.754	46.954
53.334	5.457	-4.449	58.791	48.885
48.968	1.459	7.679	50.427	56.647
44.949	-3.891	7.004	41.058	51.953
57.018	4.503	3.221	61.521	60.239
50.157	3.868	3.450	54.025	53.607
44.517	-0.647	-2.469	43.870	42.048
48.753	-11.371	-4.265	37.382	44.488

Table 27.1 – Data for Scenario 1

Figure 27.2 – Regression Analysis for Scenario 1, r-squared = 0.15

Conclusions: If using r^2 to judge correlation, this analysis leads to the **incorrect** conclusion that the two measurement systems are not correlated when we know in fact that they are correlated because we created them to be so.

Scenario 2:
- As in [Nachtsheim], each true value is multiplied by 10.
- Measurement errors are identical to scenario 1. That is, no new random numbers were generated.

Figure 27.3 illustrates the resulting linear regression analysis from scenario 2.

Figure 27.3 – Regression Analysis for Scenario 2, r-squared = 0.98

Conclusion: In this case, r^2 leads us to the **correct** conclusion that the measurement systems are in fact correlated. It is worth reiterating that in both scenarios 1 and 2 the measurement systems are unbiased, linear, and subject only to random measurement error – i.e. correlated, yet the analysis led to opposite conclusions. Further, the customer and supplier measurement systems are identical in scenarios 1 and 2 – the exact same random numbers were used for measurement error.

Scenario 3:
- This scenario is identical to scenario 2 except that a 10-unit bias is added to the supplier's measurements. In this scenario, we know that the measurement systems are **not** correlated because of the added bias.

Figure 27.4 illustrates the resulting linear regression analysis from scenario 3.

123

Figure 27.4 – Regression Analysis for Scenario 3, r-squared = 0.98

Conclusion: Again, use of r^2 to judge correlation leads us to a wrong conclusion. In this case, we **incorrectly** conclude that the measurement correlation is acceptable when in fact we know the supplier's measurement system has a 10-unit bias.

Scenario 4:
- The customer measurement system is similar to scenario 1, except that the measurement error is only 20% of that in scenario 1.
- Supplier measurement system also has random error 20% of that in scenario 1 and, in addition, has a linearity error.

$$m_{c,i} = t_i + 0.2e_{c,i}$$

$$m_{s,i} = 1.3t_i + 0.2e_{s,i}$$

Figure 27.5 illustrates the resulting linear regression analysis from scenario 4.

Figure 27.5 – Regression Analysis for Scenario 4, r-squared = 0.93

Conclusion: R^2 again shows strong correlation, leading us to the **incorrect** conclusion that the measurement systems are well correlated.

Observations:
- While the measurement errors, and hence measurement systems, are identical between the scenarios 1 and 2, the r^2 value in scenario 1 is a paltry 0.15 while that in scenario 2 is a healthy 0.98.
    - While the measurement systems in the two scenarios are identical, in scenario 1 we would conclude that the measurement systems are not correlated while in scenario 2 we would conclude they are very well correlated.
        - This results from using the r^2 value as the basis for judging correlation.

- Scenario 3 adds a systematic bias to the supplier's measurement system. Use of r^2 **incorrectly** leads to the conclusion that the measurement systems are well correlated.
- Scenario 4 simulates a linearity problem with the supplier's measurement system. Again, use of r^2 lead to the **erroneous** conclusion of good correlation.
- The astute reader might raise the following objections.
  - The regression output contains much more information than simply r^2 and this additional information may be used to identify the stated problems. I agree with this statement and, if all practitioners exhibited this understanding, the practice of using r^2 to evaluate measurement correlation would be less problematic. In practice, however, I have too often seen r^2 used as the **only** indicator of correlation when regression is employed.
  - In some cases, for example a bias that is large compared to the random component of measurement error, a quick glance at the data would point out the problem. Again, if all practitioners would employ such techniques I would agree. From a practical standpoint, I've seen many instances wherein the analysis is completed by rote and judgment of correlation rests solely on the r^2 value.

Semi-quantitative analysis:

[Devore, pp. 462 - 465] provides the following:

$$r^2 = 1 - \frac{SSE}{SST}$$

$$SSE = \sum (y_i - \hat{y}_i)^2 = Error\ Sum\ of\ Squares$$

$$SST = \sum (y_i - \bar{y})^2 = Total\ Sum\ of\ Squares$$

SSE consists of the squared differences between the actual and predicted y_i values. Every measurand (part being measured) has a true value which we can only approximate by measuring. Assuming no systematic bias in either measurement system being evaluated, in this case customer's and supplier's, the difference between actual and predicted $(y_i - \hat{y}_i)$ is due entirely to measurement error in one or both of the measurement systems. Assuming constant variance for measurement error across the range of interest (typically tolerance interval), SSE should be roughly the same magnitude, subject only to random sampling error, whether the sample being measured contains only values clustered tightly around nominal or covers the entire tolerance range. The assumption of constant measurement error/variance is common in practice as measurement systems are engineered in a manner to make it true. Contrarily, SST deals with the deviation from the grand mean rather than from the predicted value. Clearly a sample with all values clustered around nominal will have small differences between observed values and the mean and hence a much smaller SST than one that covers the entire tolerance range. The expression for r^2 forms a ratio between SSE and SST. Constant measurement error means the SSE term in the numerator is of the same magnitude regardless of sample chosen while SST in the denominator is highly dependent upon chosen sample. The ratio SSE/SST will vary dramatically as the range in the sample changes. Looked at another way, SSE consists only of measurement error (this is strictly true in the model, approximately true in real life) while SST includes part-to-part variability. Under the assumption of constant variance for measurement error, SSE is independent of sample range while SST increases quickly as the part-to-part variability (sample range) increases. **As such, r^2 is often more dependent on the sample chosen than actual measurement error in the systems being studied and is at best an indirect indicator of measurement correlation.**

Looking at the situation a little further we see that r^2 depends on the relative difference between measurement error and part-to-part variability. r^2 is not a good indicator for measurement correlation since it can be influenced by choosing a sample with more or less part-to-part variability independent of measurement systems. That is, one can arbitrarily make measurement systems look good or bad simply by choosing a different sample.

One can get the same result as in scenario 2 by keeping the true values from scenario 1 and dividing the measurement errors by 10 rather than multiplying the true values by 10. This is shown in figure 27.6.

Figure 27.6 – Same true values, all measurement errors divided by 10, r-squared = 0.98

Figure 27.6 shows us an identical r^2 value to that in figure 9 and the regression equation has the same slope, with the y-intercept different by a factor of 10 as expected.

[Nachtsheim] also shows in scenarios 3 and 4 that r^2 is insensitive to bias between the measurement systems and non-linearity of one measurement system. That is, r^2 will often fail to detect bias and non-linearity problems. Customer and supplier measurements for scenarios 2-4 are tabulated at the end of this article for reference.

Conclusions:

- The value of r^2 is heavily influenced by part-to-part variation in the sample chosen and hence is not a direct indicator of measurement correlation between two pieces of measurement equipment.
  - R^2 can be improved by choosing a sample with more part-to-part variability even if the measurement systems are not changed.
  - Low part-to-part variability will result in low r^2 even if the measurement systems are very well correlated with one another.

Recommendations:

- Use a different method than regression/r^2 for comparing correlation between pieces of measurement equipment.
  - The methods in [Nachtsheim] are appropriate.
  - I have found a control chart using the paired differences to be useful. This is discussed further in the next chapter.
- If regression is required, orthogonal regression is preferable to standard linear regression.
- Sometimes our customers are adamant about using regression, particularly r^2, to compare measurement systems or there is another driver pushing us in this direction. When that is the case:
  - When possible, choose a sample that represents the entire tolerance interval. This method relates part-to-part variability in the sample to a meaningful quantity (tolerance) for the analysis.
  - As an alternative, choose the sample to represent the full 6 sigma spread of the process. Similar to tolerance, 6 sigma of process spread is a meaningful quantity for the analysis.
  - Look past r^2 for other issues with the measurement system(s).
    - Use paired data to look for a bias between measurement systems.

- Examine the data for non-linearity in one or both measurement systems. Methods for this are outside the scope of this chapter.
- Examine the standard deviation about the regression line. The value of this standard deviation provides an idea of the spread of the differences between measured values.

Orthogonal regression:

Some sources recommend the use of orthogonal regression when both the independent and dependent variables contain measurement error. Minitab statistical software provides orthogonal regression as an option. Orthogonal regression does not provide an r^2 value, thereby avoiding the possibility of misinterpretation of this statistic. Rather, it accepts the measurement systems as equivalent if the confidence interval for the intercept includes zero and the confidence interval for the slope includes 1. Using scenarios 1-4 above shows us the following:

- Orthogonal regression correctly accepts that the measurement systems are equivalent for scenarios 1, 2.
- Orthogonal regression incorrectly accepts the measurement systems as being equivalent when a 10-unit bias is added to the supplier's measurement system in scenario 2. The correct answer would be to reject the equivalence of the measurement systems.
- Orthogonal regression correctly rejected equivalence of the measurement systems when a non-linearity of the form in [Nachtsheim] is added to the supplier's measurement system.

Orthogonal regression resulted in the correct conclusion for 3 of the 4 instances. Use of r^2 to judge correlation led to the correct conclusion in only 1 of 4 instances.

Customer Scenario 2	Supplier Scenario 2	Customer Scenario 3	Supplier Scenario 3	Customer Scenario 4	Supplier Scenario 4
449.223	457.115	449.223	467.115	44.8476	59.9251
569.342	572.461	569.342	582.461	56.2414	74.1533
453.817	459.364	453.817	469.364	44.7904	59.6917
485.011	477.756	485.011	487.756	48.9992	61.9491
473.959	464.979	473.959	474.979	48.3778	60.506
517.677	520.337	517.677	530.337	51.1384	67.3895
486.173	499.316	486.173	509.316	47.9366	65.3546
578.561	571.012	578.561	581.012	57.9452	73.7655
489.044	482.756	489.044	492.756	49.3948	62.6614
421.534	413.67	421.534	423.67	42.4468	53.432
480.79	478.463	480.79	488.463	48.518	62.3446
480.758	479.686	480.758	489.686	47.4746	61.8633
534.951	532.146	534.951	542.146	53.7302	69.1472
550.104	545.04	550.104	555.04	55.1728	70.6144
422.534	422.117	422.534	432.117	42.4138	54.9583
527.75	520.987	527.75	530.987	52.678	67.187
538.423	534.399	538.423	544.399	53.5706	69
540.832	527.032	540.832	537.032	54.8244	68.067
538.797	528.891	538.797	538.891	54.4254	68.4444
491.139	497.359	491.139	507.359	49.2598	65.1942
445.599	456.494	445.599	466.494	44.1708	59.8345
574.683	573.401	574.683	583.401	57.9186	74.7676
505.438	505.02	505.438	515.02	50.9306	65.8941
444.523	442.701	444.523	452.701	44.3876	57.3783
476.159	483.265	476.159	493.265	46.4788	62.5259

Table 27.2: Data for scenarios 2-4

28 Control Charts for Monitoring Measurement System Correlation

The previous chapter explained the pitfalls of using linear regression to evaluate measurement correlation between two pieces of measurement equipment, in this case supplier and customer measurements. Orthogonal regression, while more often leading to the correct conclusion than standard linear regression, still failed to detect a bias between measurement systems.

This article will illustrate how standard control chart methodology can provide a simple, straightforward method for comparing measurement systems and, further, for monitoring that correlation over time.

Control chart methods, using paired data, include the following advantages:
- Control charts are well-known and easy to use.
- Control charts provide a graphical illustration of the agreement between measurement systems.
- Plotting the differences between paired deviations makes it easy to spot a bias or non-linearity.
- Correlation can be monitored over time by plotting subsequent values on the same control chart and examining the data for trends.
- Control charts make it easy to visually compare new data to past performance since newly added data automatically show up on the right-hand side of the chart.

The data from scenarios 1-4 in **"Use of Linear Regression analysis and r^2 for determining correlation of measurement system can be misleading and result in wrong decisions"** are analyzed below using control charts for the paired difference of measurements. Table 1 from the referenced article is duplicated below as table 28.1 with a column added to illustrate the paired difference.

True Value	Customer Msmnt Error	Supplier Msmnt Error	Customer Measured Value	Supplier Measured Value	Paired Difference (customer minus supplier)
44.997	-0.747	7.145	44.250	52.142	-7.892
57.627	-6.928	-3.809	50.699	53.818	-3.119
45.973	-5.913	-0.366	40.060	45.607	-5.547
48.003	4.981	-2.274	52.984	45.729	7.255
46.414	9.819	0.839	56.233	47.253	8.98
52.397	-6.293	-3.633	46.104	48.764	-2.66
49.298	-6.807	6.336	42.491	55.634	-13.143
57.767	0.891	-6.658	58.658	51.109	7.549
48.414	4.904	-1.384	53.318	47.03	6.288
41.860	2.934	-4.930	44.794	36.93	7.864
47.640	4.390	2.063	52.030	49.703	2.327
48.677	-6.012	-7.084	42.665	41.593	1.072
53.260	2.351	-0.454	55.611	52.806	2.805
54.848	1.624	-3.440	56.472	51.408	5.064
42.093	1.604	1.187	43.697	43.28	0.417
52.872	-0.970	-7.733	51.902	45.139	6.763
54.114	-2.717	-6.741	51.397	47.373	4.024
53.342	7.412	-6.388	60.754	46.954	13.8
53.334	5.457	-4.449	58.791	48.885	9.906
48.968	1.459	7.679	50.427	56.647	-6.22
44.949	-3.891	7.004	41.058	51.953	-10.895
57.018	4.503	3.221	61.521	60.239	1.282
50.157	3.868	3.450	54.025	53.607	0.418
44.517	-0.647	-2.469	43.870	42.048	1.822
48.753	-11.371	-4.265	37.382	44.488	-7.106

Table 28.1 – Data for Scenario 1

Scenario 1:

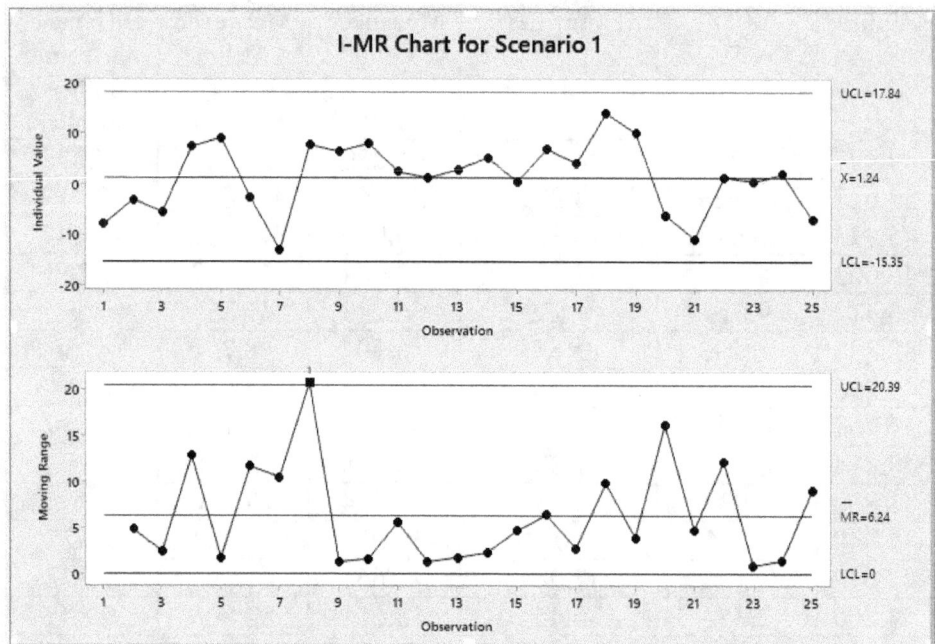

Figure 28.1 – X and MR chart for difference between customer and supplier measurements for Scenario 1

We can immediately glean the following from figure 28.1:

- The mean difference between the customer and supplier measurement systems is 1.24 units.
- The control limits for the x-value include zero and further are nearly centered around zero.
- One point on the MR chart is o.o.c. (out of control) which would lead to an investigation which in this case would fail to find an assignable cause.
- Standard deviation of the difference between the customer and supplier measurements can be estimated from the average MR value using standard control chart methods. In this case the estimated standard deviation of the differences is 5.53.
- Note that all tests for o.o.c. conditions were active in Minitab using default k-values.

134

In addition, the control chart gives us the option to project the limits forward and use it for ongoing monitoring of measurement correlation. This would provide the following advantages:

- Use of smaller sample size to monitor correlation in the future. Since the control chart defines "normal correlation" by use of control limits, a single measurement or small group of measurements can be used to monitor correlation over time.
- The control chart automatically includes history over time by virtue of adding new data to the existing control chart.

Note that x-bar and R charts may be used, and in many cases, may be preferred, instead of X and MR charts. The concepts are the same. X and MR is used for ease of illustration and, in my experience, it is desired to conduct ongoing monitoring with a minimum burden for data collection.

Scenario 2:

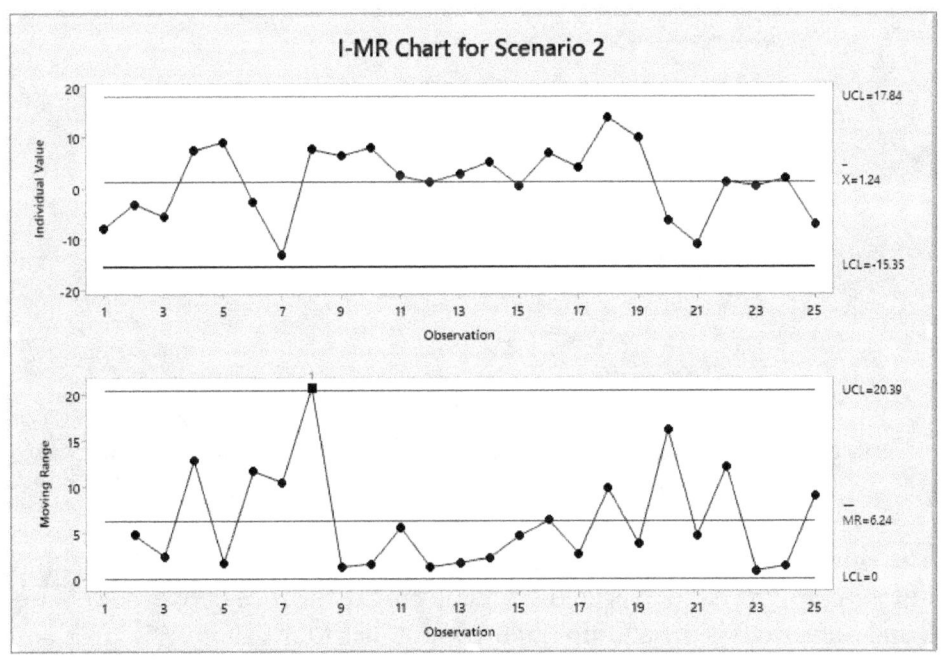

Figure 28.2 – X and MR chart for difference between customer and supplier measurements for Scenario 2

A benefit of this type of analysis becomes immediately apparent. The control charts for scenario 2 look identical to those for scenario 1 – **as they should**. Remember, the only difference between scenario 1 and 2 is that the unknown "true" value was multiplied by a factor of 10. The measurement systems, and each individual measurement error, were identical.

Scenario 3:

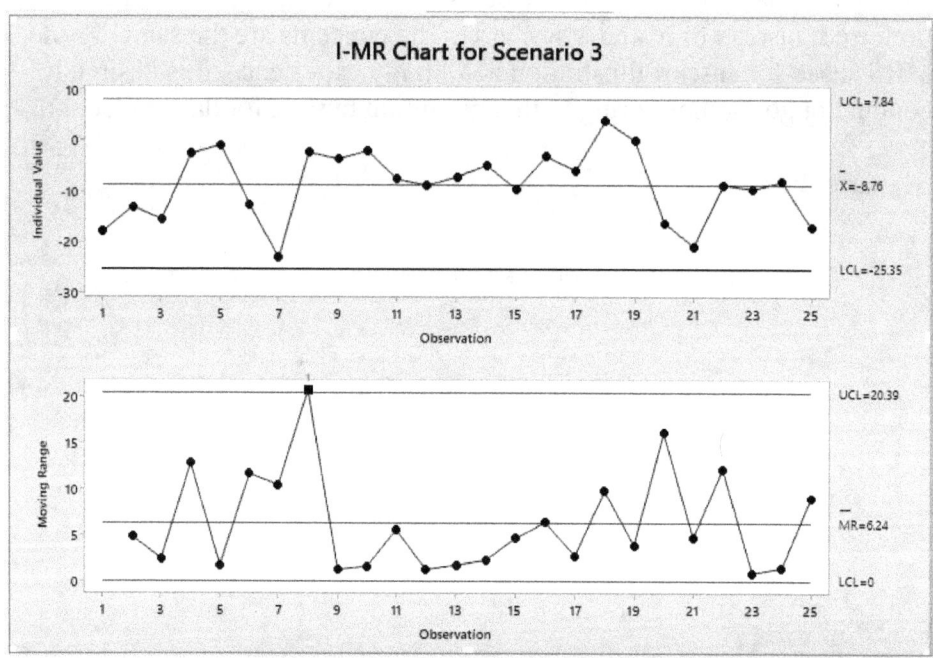

Figure 28.3 – X and MR chart for difference between customer and supplier measurements for Scenario 3

The control charts are very similar to those for scenarios 1 and 2. Again, this similarity is to be expected since the only difference between scenario 2 and scenario 3 is the addition of a 10-unit bias to the supplier's

136

measurement system. This bias becomes evident by comparing the mean difference of 1.24 in scenario 2 to the mean difference of -8.76 in scenario 3. Obviously, a mean difference of -8.76 is larger in magnitude than a mean difference of 1.24. Having said this, how do we determine whether this difference is significant? From a statistical standpoint, a paired t-test leads to the conclusion that the difference of 1.24 **is not** significant ($p = 0.376$) while the difference of -8.76 **is** significant ($p = 0.000$). From a practical standpoint, discussions between the customer and supplier would determine what difference causes a concern.

Scenario 4:

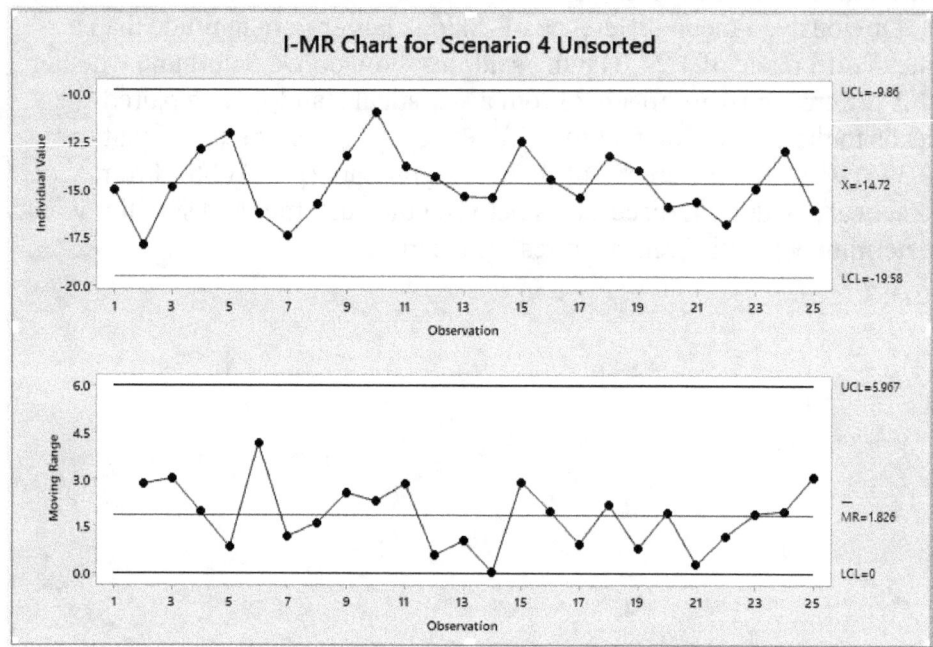

Figure 28.4 - X and MR chart for difference between customer and supplier measurements for Scenario 4

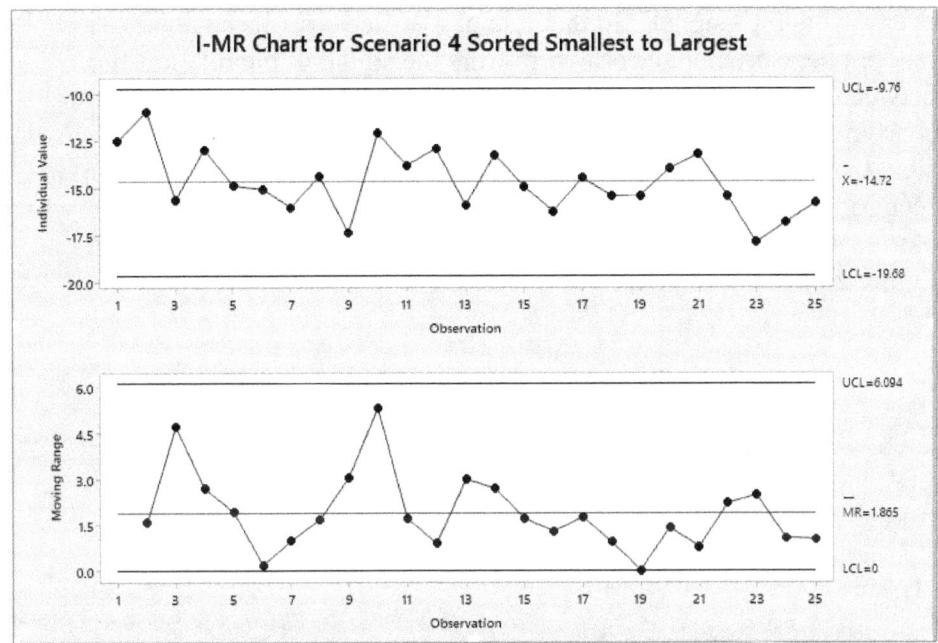

Figure 28.5 – X and MR charts for difference between customer and supplier measurements for Scenario 4. Top graph is in order measured, bottom graph sorted from smallest to largest based on customer measurements

The mean difference in scenario 4 is -14.72. A paired t-test again shows the mean difference statistically different than zero (p = 0.000) – that is, we conclude the measurement systems are not correlated by virtue of a non-zero bias between them.

Two graphs are presented for scenario 4. The top graph is plotted in the order in which measurements were taken (random) while the bottom graph is plotted from smallest to largest based on the customer measurements. One would anticipate the graph plotted smallest to largest to show a trend, given the stated non-linearity. While it can be argued that the graph hints at a trend, none of the o.o.c. conditions were triggered so it would clearly be premature to conclude a trend based on the chart. Why did the expected trend not exhibit? Similar to the problems with r^2 in scenario 1, the "noise"

139

overpowers the "signal". In the case of r^2 in scenario 1, the noise of random measurement error overpowers the signal of the relationship between customer and supplier measurements. In the case of the control chart in scenario 4, the noise of random measurement error overpowers the signal provided by the nonlinearity. Example: if the nonlinearity term in scenario 4 were increased from 1.3 to 2, the trend becomes apparent, when plotted smallest to largest (customer measurements), as illustrated in Figure 28.6.

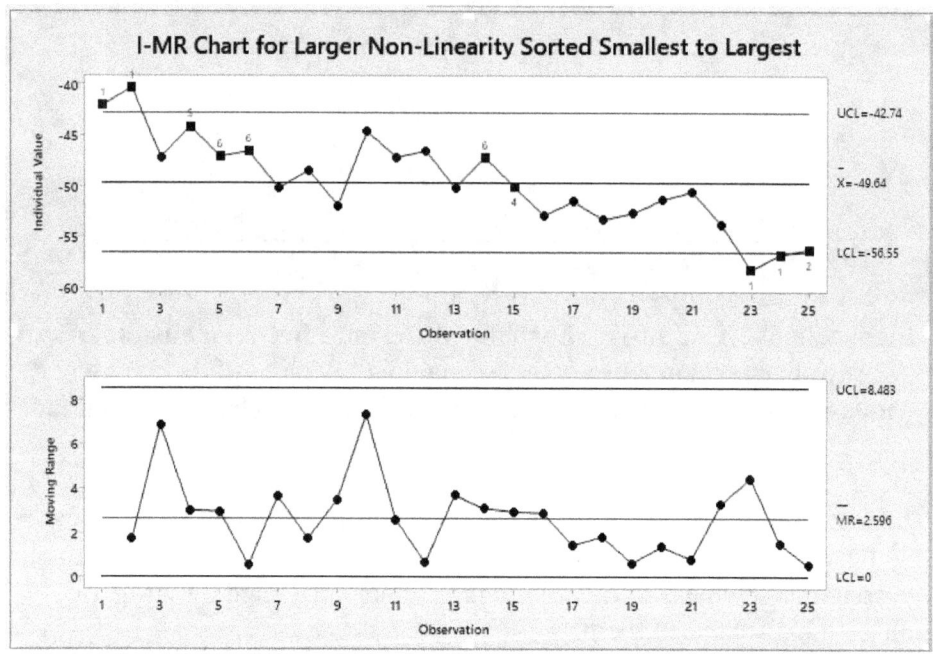

Figure 28.6 – X and MR chart for difference between customer and supplier measurements with non-linearity term increased from 1.3 to 2, sorted smallest to largest based on customer measurements

Summary: Use of control charts to evaluate measurement correlation between 2 pieces of measurement equipment, combined with a paired t-test, resulted in the correct conclusion for all 4 scenarios, proving more robust than either r^2 or orthogonal regression for the stated examples. Note that the paired t-test identified the bias in scenario 4 while the control

140

chart failed to identify the non-linearity until it became more extreme. The advantages of control charts also include:

- Use for ongoing monitoring by extending the control limits into the future.
- Reduced sample size for ongoing monitoring from leveraging the control limits calculated in the initial study.
- Ease of interpretation – SPC is a well-understood technique
- New data can be added to the chart as it is obtained.
  - The new data can be readily compared visually with previous data.
  - The new data is immediately apparent from the chart, being the last plotted.
    - Contrast this with adding new data to an existing data set with regression analysis. The regression plot does not indicate the order in which the data was collected/plotted.

29 Cpk and Ppk, similarities, differences, when to use

$$Cpk = \min\left[\frac{USL - \bar{\bar{x}}}{3s_c}, \frac{\bar{\bar{x}} - LSL}{3s_c}\right]$$

$$Ppk = \min\left[\frac{USL - \bar{\bar{x}}}{3s_p}, \frac{\bar{\bar{x}} - LSL}{3s_p}\right]$$

These formulae are very similar, in fact at quick examination they are identical. However, there is a slight but very important difference signified by the subscript for the standard deviation estimate. What is this difference and what does it mean? The standard deviation for Cpk is estimated from control chart parameters while the standard deviation for Ppk uses the classical estimate from statistics. Specifically,

$$s_c = \frac{\bar{R}}{d_2}$$

$$s_p = \sqrt{\frac{\Sigma(x_i - \bar{\bar{x}})^2}{n - 1}}$$

Note that the expression for s_c assumes use of X-bar and R charts. Use of other types of control charts, for example X-bar and S or X and MR would change the expression according to the type of chart used, but standard deviation is still estimated from the control chart. [Bothe] refers to the standard deviation estimate used for Cpk as short-term process spread and that used for Ppk as long-term process spread. Minitab statistical software uses the same estimates for Cpk and Ppk shown above as can be verified via the Minitab help menu.

So, how big of a deal is this subscript in the formulae? An example might be most instructive. The following Minitab sixpack is based on real data

142

from a previous job. The specific data is proprietary and has been coded. All of the lessons to be learned from the analysis are identical to the real-life situation. This was part of a process validation by a supplier in the medical device industry. The validation protocol acceptance criteria stated a minimum Cpk of 1.33. The supplier recommended passing the validation because the calculated Cpk is 2.17. I refused to approve the validation. What is wrong with the supplier's recommendation to approve?

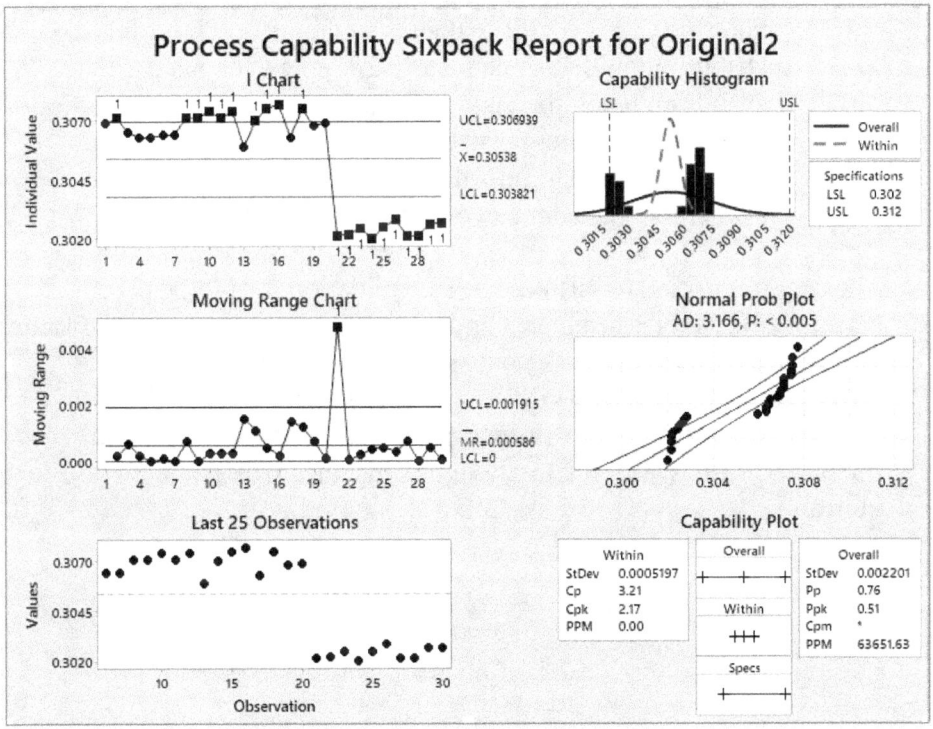

Figure 29.1 – Validation 6-Pack

There are a number of problems with the validation. First, a short explanation of validation. Process validation is intended to demonstrate via objective evidence that the process is capable of consistently producing product meeting specification. Problems with the recommendation include:

- The control chart shows a distinct mean shift.

143

- The histogram is clearly bimodal.
- The normal probability plot shows a non-normal distribution.
- Ppk is 0.51, predicting nonconforming product.
- The dashed line distribution on the histogram represents the predicted distribution using control chart statistics – that is, the Cpk equivalent distribution. It is quickly observed that this calculated distribution excludes the majority of the actual data. Cpk clearly misrepresents the data and, in fact, implies much greater process capability than is in fact true. The solid line distribution on that same histogram represents the predicted distribution using the classical estimate of standard deviation – that is, the Ppk equivalent distribution. This estimate is quite conservative in that the tails of the distribution extend a considerable distance beyond the actual data.

The supplier initially insisted that the validation should be accepted because Cpk met requirements and there were no actual nonconforming products. I then modified the data set to include (simulated) nonconforming product as illustrated below. **The Cpk is still above 1.33 (2.10 to be specific) even though actual nonconforming product is now included in the results.** Clearly in this instance Cpk is not a good indicator.

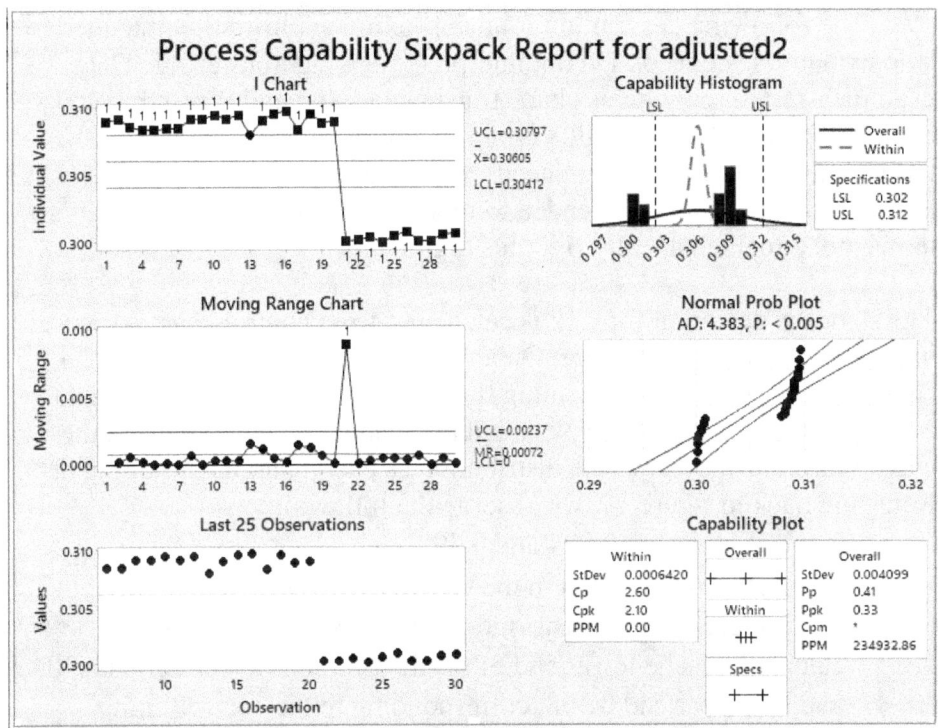

Figure 29.2 – Validation 6-Pack Modified To Include Nonconforming Product

If a process is in a state of statistical control, Cpk and Ppk will be similar. If the two indicators differ by a significant amount, the prudent QE or ME will figure out why. In this particular case, the supplier identified a process adjustment made in the middle of the validation run to explain the mean shift. They made the argument that the process is capable and the process adjustment is in their control. I believed this to be true, however the validation did not "demonstrate via objective evidence that the process was capable of consistently producing conforming product". The validation was repeated and passed without a problem.

So, why does Cpk overestimate capability in an instance like this and make the process look better than it really is? Let's refer back to Figure

145

29.2. The following description is an approximate illustration intended to help explain the concept. Do not interpret it as a rigorous proof. The example uses an individuals chart. If using an x-bar and R or x-bar and s chart, the control limits would pertain to **averages** rather than to individuals and the discussion needs to change accordingly. Again, this is an approximate example intended to represent the situation in layman's terms, not a mathematically rigorous argument.

The standard deviation for Cpk is calculated from control chart statistics, in particular the average range. On an individuals chart, Cpk views the control limits for X as representing the width of the distribution of data expected from the process. Ppk calculates standard deviation using the classic formula and views the distribution as encompassing all of the data. Referring back to figure 19, we observe the following:

- Control limits are 0.304 and 0.308.
- The dotted distribution in the Capability Histogram graph (upper right) represents the distribution resulting from the Cpk calculation. The lower end of the distribution (lower tail) is 0.304 and the upper end 0.308, corresponding to the control limits.
- The actual data points range from 0.3 to 0.31, considerably outside the Cpk-predicted distribution.
- The solid distribution in the Capability Histogram graph (upper right) represents the distribution resulting from the Ppk calculation. The lower end of the distribution (lower tail) is 0.294 and the upper end 0.318, capturing all of the data.

Since Cpk estimates standard deviation using the ranges between successive measurements (based on the average moving range in an X and MR chart), the majority of small moving ranges dominates the single large moving range when the process shifts lower. The calculation of standard deviation used in Ppk, however, uses the deviation of each point from the overall mean as can be seen from the formula. A quick review of figure 19 will show that the difference between successive points is almost always less than the difference of the points from the overall mean. As mentioned,

146

this is an approximate illustration only. A statistician can find criticisms of the illustration from a mathematical standpoint. If it helps the reader conceptually understand the difference between Cpk and Ppk, its purpose is served despite the lack of mathematical rigor.

Specifically:
- The estimate of standard deviation for Cpk does include the one large moving range. This large value tends to increase standard deviation estimate but is dominated by the 28 small moving ranges.
- The Ppk estimate extends beyond the actual data in the example. However, the main point is the same – Ppk estimate is considerably lower (indicating worse capability) than Cpk when the data exhibits a mean shift as in the example.
- The important point from the figure is that the moving range, MR, used to estimate standard deviation for Cpk is dominated by the majority of small moving ranges, resulting in an underestimate of standard deviation. The classical estimate of standard deviation used for Ppk more explicitly includes the entire range of the data.

I have observed that in practice, when Cpk and Ppk differ by a significant amount, Ppk more often provides a conservative (i.e. lower) estimate of process capability. However, this is not always the case. When the calculated control limits are too wide, for example data points clustered around the mean, Cpk can provide a more conservative estimate. It is worth noting that data points clustered around the mean represents an out-of-control condition. As a general rule, Ppk is the more robust estimator but as has been promoted throughout this book, a competent and conscientious engineer will strive to understand the reason for any unusual results and make a well thought out and defensible decision regarding which indicator is most appropriate in a given situation.

I recently learned a 'trick' in Minitab to make Cpk become more similar to Ppk. If parts were chosen randomly instead of in time order, setting the subgroup size equal to the total sample, rather than using a subgroup size of 1, will instruct Minitab to calculate Cpk in a more similar manner to

Ppk. Example: if we have a total of 30 measurements, set the subgroup size equal to 30. Advantages to this approach include:

- Trends on control charts, using a subgroup size of 1, may be misleading if the sample is random rather than in time order of manufacture.
- Since the difference between Cpk and Ppk in this scenario is smaller, we are less likely to make a wrong decision.

Given this, I would still use Ppk. Why?

- Doing so negates the need to remember the 'trick' and, if someone else performs the analysis with a subgroup size of 1, Cpk could be quite misleading as explained above.
- When Cpk and Ppk differ, that in itself can be a clue to look further at the data. I feel obligated to state here that it's almost always a good idea to look at the data further even when Cpk and Ppk are in reasonable agreement; in practice this doesn't happen as often as it should.

30 Myth: Sampling 10% provides the same assurance for any lot size

Reality: Sample size does not scale with lot size in this manner.

An example of the myth would be that sampling 10 pieces from a 100-piece lot provides the same quality assurance level as sampling 100 pieces from a 1000-piece lot.

Assume:
- $c = 0$ sampling plan, that is accept the lot if zero nonconforming units are found in the sample, reject the lot if 1 or more nonconforming units are found in the sample.
- Both lots contain 5% nonconforming units.

The sampling plan has a 58% chance of accepting the 100-piece lot, yet less than a 1% chance of accepting the 1000-piece lot – even though both lots have the same 5% nonconforming rate. These statistics were calculated using the hypergeometric distribution.

A quick review of ANSI Z1.4 will confirm that sample size does not scale proportionally to lot size for a constant quality assurance level.

A useful way to think of it is if a lot is 1% nonconforming, there is a 1/100 chance of finding a nonconformance each time a sample is pulled. This is independent of lot size – since we are dealing with a constant 1% nonconforming a 1000-piece lot will contain 10 nonconforming units while a 100-piece lot will contain only a single nonconforming unit. A sample size of 10 represents 10 opportunities to find one or more nonconforming units while a sample size of 100 has ten times as many opportunities to find one or more nonconforming units. **Important note**: this explanation assumes that the probability of finding a nonconforming unit stays constant throughout the sample. This is only strictly true if we are sampling with replacement, that is each sample is placed back into the lot after inspection and may be randomly pulled again in subsequent sampling. It becomes approximately true as the lot size gets large. While it's important to understand this assumption and that the statistics are not exact for sampling without replacement, it is useful to illustrate the general concept that sample size does not scale proportionally with lot size.

Example 30.1: (based on actual event, details changed to protect proprietary information): A company manufactures expensive parts. Lot size is 200. [Squeglia] indicates a sample size of 20 for a 1.0 AQL. Accept if all 20 are conforming, reject if any nonconforming product is found. Because the parts are so expensive, failing 200 parts at one time is undesirable so it is naively suggested that inspecting 5 parts per 50 produced and accepting or rejecting 50 at a time is an acceptable alternative. After all, if we inspect 5 parts from every group of 50 we are still inspecting 20 parts out of every 200 produced. We only have to sort or rework 50 at a time rather than 200 and are still inspecting the same number of parts, so everyone is happy, right? Can you see the problem here? It's a classic example of incorrectly assuming that sample size scales proportionally with lot size.

Let's look at a specific example. Assume 8% nonconforming. In a lot size of 50, this is 4 nonconforming parts and in a lot size of 200, we have 16 nonconforming parts. The proper analysis method for this situation entails use of the hypergeometric distribution. We are asking the two questions:
1. If we have 4 nonconforming parts in a group of 50 parts, what is the chance of randomly sampling 5 consecutive conforming parts? Note: the lot of 50 only passes if all 5 sampled parts are conforming.
2. If we have 16 nonconforming parts in a group of 200 parts, what is the chance of randomly sampling 20 consecutive conforming parts?

The answer to question #1 is an approximately 65% chance of accepting the lot. The answer to question #2 is an approximately 17% chance of accepting the lot. By changing the lot size and proportionally sampling, we have increased the chance of accepting an 8% nonconforming rate almost 4x. Now, you might say, but there are 4x as many 50-piece lots as

200-piece lots so a larger absolute number of 50-piece lots are rejected. Does this come out as a wash? To explore this question, we will have to use another concept, Average Outgoing Quality (AOQ). This concept assumes 100% effective inspection in the QC audit and any follow-up sorting or rework of nonconforming product. Since this assumption is typically not true, the AOQ formula below is an approximation. Nonetheless, it is widely used and accepted. [Juran, p. 46.10] provides:

$$AOQ = p(P_a)$$

AOQ = Average Outgoing Quality
p = proportion nonconforming
P_a = Probability of acceptance for a series of lots arriving to the QC audit with proportion nonconforming equal to p.

In words, this simply states that any lots which are rejected are sorted or reworked and shipped with perfect quality. Those lots that are accepted by the sampling plan, despite having nonconforming units, are shipped with all nonconforming units included. AOQ is often graphed as a continuous curve. However, because of the small lot size used in the example, a discrete approach is required. The figure below compares AOQ, as a function of quality coming to inspection, for both a sampling plan of 20 out of 200 and a sampling plan of 5 out of 50.

Since a single unit must either be conforming or nonconforming, only certain values for % nonconforming are possible in a 50-piece lot – 0%, 2%, 4%, . . . 100%. For the sake of simplicity, these are the only values of % nonconforming evaluated and graphed in figure 20.

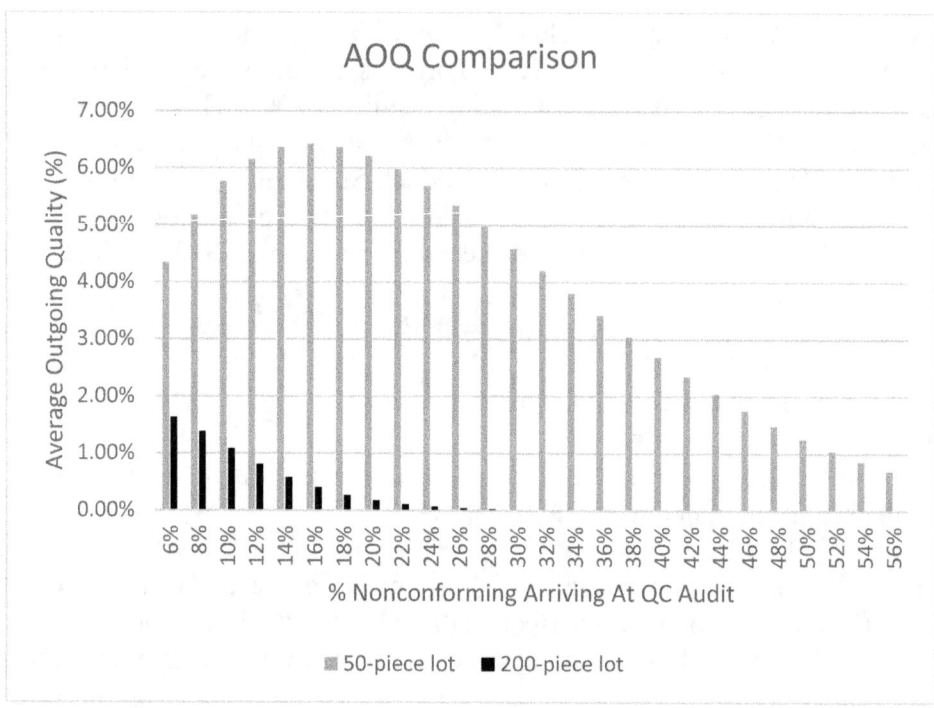

Figure 30.1 – AOQ Curves for 50 and 200-piece Lots

Some notable conclusions from the graph:

- If perfect quality arrives at QC audit, perfect quality is shipped to the customer.
- There is a maximum for AOQ for each sampling plan, this is referred to as the Average Outgoing Quality Limit (AOQL).
- As quality arriving at the QC audit gets worse, AOQ increases for a period of time, then decreases. This is due to the assumption of perfect sorting/rework. As the quality arriving at the QC audit gets worse, a higher and higher percentage of the lots are failed and then sorted or reworked to remove all nonconforming units. As we approach 100% of the lots failing at QC, we approach perfect quality being shipped to the customer because of the assumption of perfect sorting/rework.

152

- At each distinct value, sampling 20 pieces out of 200 provides better AOQ to the customer than sampling 5 pieces out of 50 – even though we end up inspecting the same number of total parts.
- At worst case, AOQL, sampling 5 pieces out of 50 can result in almost 6.5% nonconforming going to the customer while the AOQL for sampling 20 pieces out of 200 is approximately 1.7%. This means the outgoing quality could be up to almost 4x worse when sampling 5 pieces out of 50 compared to sampling 20 pieces out of 200.

Remember that the preceding discussion assumed we were dispositioning each group of 50 as accept or reject based on a single sample of 5. The conclusions change if this is not the case.

While the assumption of perfect QC inspection and sorting is not typically true in practice, the conclusions reached are analogous to the general situation where 100% perfect inspection and sorting are not assumed.

[Squeglia] indicates that a 1.0 AQL for a 50-piece lot requires a sample size of 13 rather than the 5 that was naively assumed. Thus, maintaining the same AQL requires us to inspect 2.6x as many parts when using 50-piece lots as when using 200-piece lots.

31 Myth: a 1.0 AQL Protects against a 1% defect rate

Reality: A 1.0% AQL means that a 1% defect rate is likely to be **accepted**. This is the opposite of protecting against a 1% defect rate. LTPD is the proper metric to use when discussing protection against a given defect rate.

In ANSI Z1.4, AQL is defined as "The AQL is the quality level that is the worst tolerable process average when a continuing series of lots is submitted for acceptance sampling." The term "tolerable" implies "acceptable". A numerical example might be helpful.

[Squeglia] provides a family of sampling plans for a 1.0 AQL. The specific sample size varies with lot size. Table 31.1 lists a few of these plans along with the percent chance of acceptance if the lot contains 1% nonconforming. The hypergeometric distribution is used to calculate % chance of accepting the lot.

Lot Size	Sample Size	% Chance of Accepting A Lot With 1% Nonconforming
100	13	87%
200	20	81%
400	29	74%

Table 31.1 – Chance of Accepting A Lot With 1% Nonconforming for Different Lot Sizes Using Sampling Plans In [Squeglia]

In all 3 examples, a 1.0 AQL has a better than 70% chance of being accepted by the 1.0 AQL sampling plan with 2 of the 3 examples having a better than 80% chance of being accepted. Rather than providing protection against a 1% defect rate, a 1.0 AQL plan will accept the majority of lots presented to it with 1% nonconforming product. [Squeglia] uses only zero acceptance number sampling plans. The chance of accepting is generally even higher when one moves away from c=0 plans. ANSI Z1.4, mentioned earlier, provides a family of sampling plans

154

with acceptance numbers equal to and greater than zero. Many of these 1.0 AQL plans have a greater than 90% chance of accepting a lot that is 1% defective.

32 Myth: If $r^2 < 0.8$, the measurement system is out of control

Reality: By now we should understand that r^2 is unrelated to whether something is in a state of statistical control.

This statement was made by a customer that was using r^2 to determine correlation between their measurement system and ours (supplier). Low r^2 is **not** proof of a lack of statistical control. r^2 and a state of statistical control as indicated on a Shewhart control chart are independent concepts. That is, r^2 can be high or low both when the measurement systems being compared are in a state of statistical control and when they are not. Admittedly it is easier to achieve a high r^2 value when the measurement systems are in a state of statistical control than when they are not, but high r^2 is possible even in the absence of statistical control.

The reader is referred to chapter 27. In that chapter, measurement error was modeled as normally distributed, random data both for the situations with high and low r^2. Normally distributed data is by definition in a state of statistical control. Since the same normally distributed measurement errors can result in both high and low r^2 values, it follows that the r^2 value does not by itself indicate whether a measurement system is in or out of control.

33 Myth: If Cpk < 1.0, the process is out of control

Reality: Low Cpk may be a clue that the process is not in a state of statistical control (i.e. "out of control"), but is not proof of a lack of control.

Consider first the formula for Cpk:

$$Cpk = Min\left[\frac{USL - \bar{\bar{x}}}{3s}, \frac{\bar{\bar{x}} - LSL}{3s}\right]$$

Where:
Min = the minimum of the two listed terms
USL = Upper Specification Limit
LSL = Lower Specification Limit
$\bar{\bar{x}}$ = the process grand average
s = standard deviation **as calculated from control chart statistics**

Control limits are calculated from (X-bar and R chart):

$$UCL = \bar{\bar{x}} + A_2\bar{R}$$
$$LCL = \bar{\bar{x}} - A_2\bar{R}$$

Where:
UCL = Upper Control Limit (used to determine whether process is in a state of statistical control)
LCL = Lower Control Limit (used to determine whether process is in a state of statistical control)
$\bar{\bar{x}}$ = the grand average of the collected (charted) data
A_2 = tabulated control chart factor
$\bar{R}$ = the average subgroup range

Consider the following situation:

157

- USL = 50
- LSL = 40
- Process grand average = 45
- Standard deviation estimated from control chart = 1
- The control chart indicates a state of statistical control
- In this situation, Cpk = 1.67

Now consider that everything stays exactly the same except the customer changes the USL to 47 and the LSL to 43. The process is still in a state of statistical control, yet Cpk has reduced from 1.67 to 0.67. A state of statistical control depends **only** on the measured data while Cpk depends directly on tolerance limits.

Note: a state of statistical control is required for Cpk to be a valid process capability index or to have the common interpretation. This is true because the standard deviation used in the formula is estimated from control chart statistics and this method of estimating standard deviation only applies when the control chart demonstrates a state of statistical control. Ppk is often used when a state of statistical control has not been achieved. Refer to chapter 29 for a more thorough explanation.

The astute reader may be asking "what about the r-chart?" since proper practice is to **always combine a chart for central tendency or mean such as x-bar or X with a chart for variability such as R or s**. The R-chart was not mentioned because the statement that "Cpk < 1.0 means a process is out of control" can be proven false without need to consider the r-chart. The bolded statement cannot be over-emphasized as ignoring the R, s, or other chart for variability is a common mistake made in Manufacturing.

34 Data transformation is often over-used/used as a crutch

Let's start out by being very clear. **Data transformation is a highly respected, very useful tool in statistics.** The intent of this chapter is not to malign data transformation, rather to highlight some poor practices observed repeatedly throughout industry. Data transformation provides so much flexibility that too many people use it as a first choice or "get out of jail free" card rather than studying a problem to identify what is really going on with the process or product.

What is data transformation? Essentially, transformation is using a mathematical function to make non-normal data look normal so that it can be analyzed using a normal distribution. Arguably the most common transformation is lognormal. The transformation is accomplished by taking the natural logarithm (or base 10 or other base) of each data point. The data, post transformation, can then be analyzed as a normal distribution to estimate % nonconforming or other parameters. A caution is in order. While individual data points are transformed back into original data by a simple exponential, transforming mean and standard deviation are considerably more complicated. Figure 34.1 is a lognormal distribution prior to transformation and figure 34.2 the same data after transformation. The change in shape from right-skewed to approximately normal is apparent.

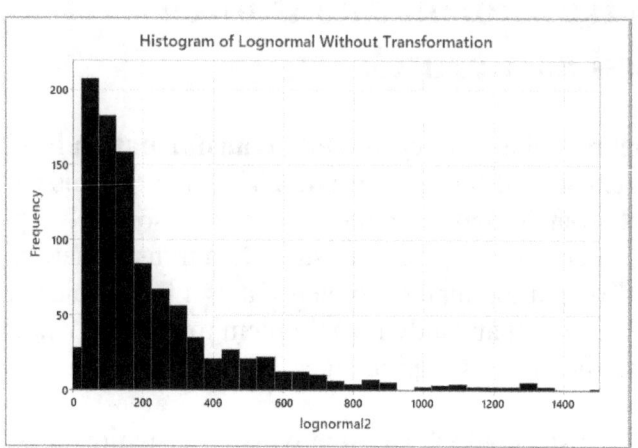

Figure 34.1 – Lognormally Distributed Data Before Transformation

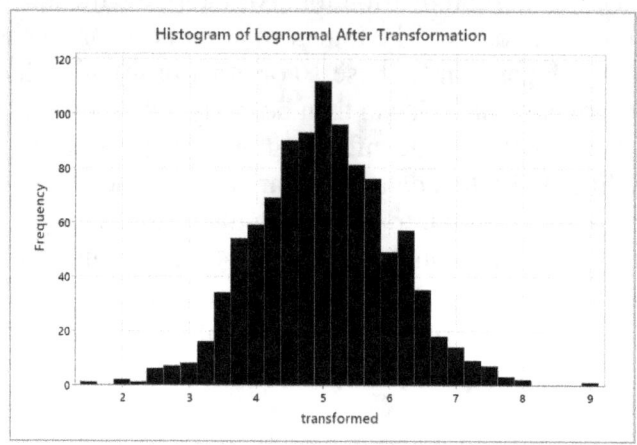

Figure 34.2 – Lognormally Distributed Data After Transformation

The normal distribution has been extensively studied and is much easier to work with than the untransformed lognormal, so why is this a problem? It becomes a problem when well-meaning practitioners transform data that should be inherently normal, yet contain an assignable cause that make them appear to be non-normal.

First, a brief explanation of a common practice in industry. Process validation protocols often include provisions along the following lines:

- Test for normality. If p-value > 0.05, accept the assumption of normality and calculate capability indices. Accept if Cpk/Ppk are greater than 1.33, reject otherwise.
- If p-value during normality test < 0.05, reject the normality assumption. Transform the data, calculate capability indices, and accept or reject as above.

The following example consists of two normal distributions, one with a mean of 50 and standard deviation of 3, the other with a mean of 61 and a standard deviation of 3 analyzed as a single distribution. How might this type of mean shift arise in practice?

- Maybe an operator made an improper machine adjustment during the validation run
- Raw material lot may have been changed and the proper machine adjustment was not made
- Parts may have been improperly mixed from two different machines.
- Etc.

The point of the example is – we have two different distributions that may be made to look like a single distribution. A Minitab capability sixpack illustrates the situation in figure 34.3, using a tolerance of 34 – 70. The data fails the normality test with a p-value on the normal probability plot of 0.027. To an experienced QE, there are a number of other problems that jump out from the sixpack including:

- Clear mean shift on the control chart.
- Indication of bimodal distribution on the histogram although it's worth noting that the mean shift is much less obvious on the histogram than the control chart.
- P-value on the normal probability plot is less than 0.05.
- Large difference between Cpk and Ppk. In fact, Cpk easily passes the 1.33 minimum requirement while Ppk clearly fails that criterion. The difference between Cpk and Ppk is explored in more

161

detail in chapter 29. It is noted here that if a process is in a state of statistical control, Cpk and Ppk will be similar. A significant difference between them is a sign that something is affecting the data that warrants further investigation.

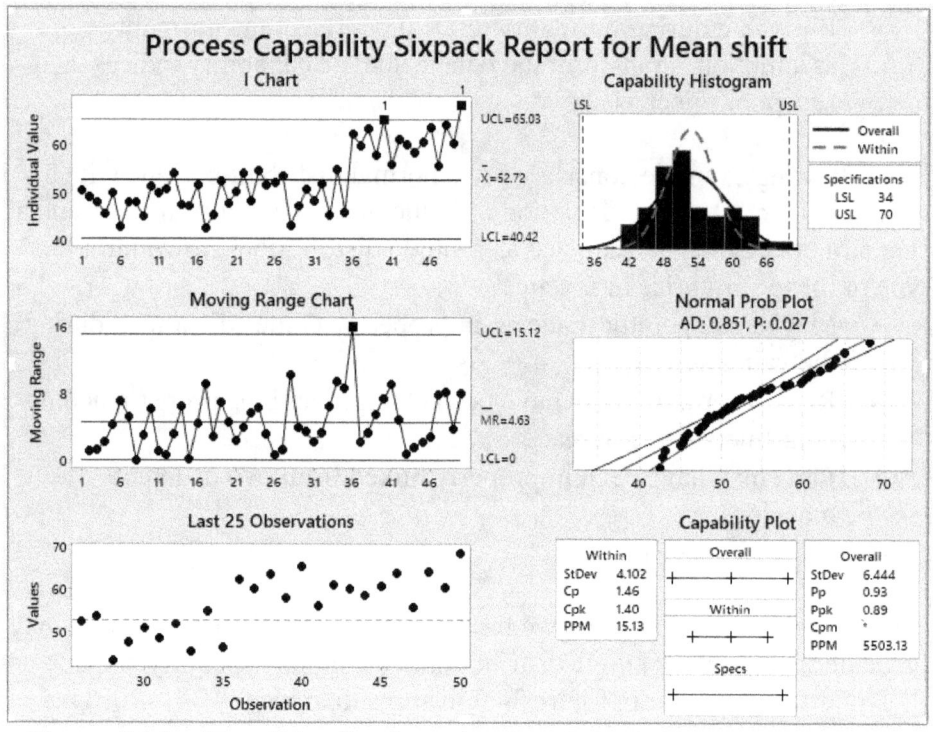

Figure 34.3 – Two Distributions Analyzed As A Single Distribution

The sixpack analysis is repeated using transformed data and illustrated in figure 34.4. The p-value after transformation is 0.778. Many procedures in industry state that if the p-value is above 0.05, the distribution may be analyzed as if it were normal. The good news in this particular instance is the control chart still shows a shift and the transformed capability analysis still indicates a low Ppk value and would drive some investigation/improvement activities. This would not always be the case.

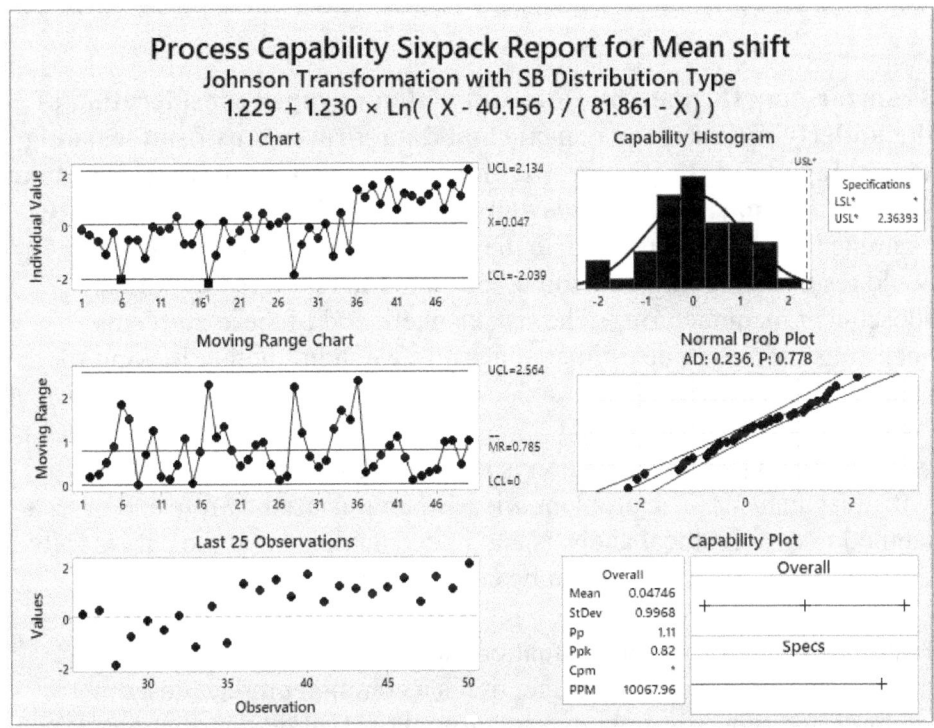

Figure 34.4 – 6-Pack Repeated After Johnson Transformation

What if the capability index had met the 1.33 Cpk/Ppk requirement? This would occur if the upper tolerance were a number higher than 70. Typical practice would be to accept and move onto other issues without further analysis. This is where we would be missing out on some very useful information. The mean shift that occurred during the run had an assignable cause. Understanding that assignable cause allows us to decide whether some action is appropriate to improve the process and reduce the chance of failure during volume production. Possible actions, depending on the cause of the mean shift could include:

- Verify machine settings when changing material lots.
- Modify procedure to prevent operator tampering with process settings.
- Track different machines separately to avoid mixing production streams and masking problems.

163

- Etc.

Transforming the data by rote, and without proper consideration of the underlying cause for non-normal data, prevents us from learning something about the process that might be much more important than whether this particular validation passes or fails. Failure to critically examine the data and investigate the cause of the bimodal distribution could result in ongoing downtime, failures, and related costs during subsequent manufacturing. The risk or likelihood of these problems occurring can't even be estimated because we didn't bother looking for the cause.

In summary, data transformation is a very useful and valid technique for statistical analysis. The problem arises when it is used by rote and/or as a method to avoid critical analysis and understanding what the data is truly trying to tell us and what might be causing the non-normal condition.

Final word: There are many situations wherein we would not expect a normal distribution. Metal fatigue life is a common product design example and typically follows a lognormal or Weibull distribution. We would be surprised to find it normal. The lognormal/Weibull distributions in this case are supported by physics and are the expected natural distributions. In such a case, data transformation is a preferred method or, given today's computing capability, one can analyze the underlying distribution (Weibull for example) directly. My personal preference is to directly use the underlying distribution, believing it to provide a better scientific understanding of the object or process under consideration. The notable exception to this is lognormal. A process example of a naturally non-normal distribution arises in the area of GD&T wherein many tolerances have a natural bound at zero. A negative result is impossible so, if the process is highly capable, measurements will be stacked close to zero and will naturally be right-skewed and more exponential or lognormal than normal.

35 Myth: 95/95 always refers to 95% confidence and 95% reliability

Reality: In many cases it is more accurate to say 95% confidence and 95% conformance.

This myth can be stated more generally as XX/YY always refers to XX% confidence and YY% reliability.

In this chapter, I need to indulge my training as a Reliability Engineer. The confidence/reliability terminology is so ubiquitous that it's probably not realistic to change it. It's important for users, however, to understand that there is a distinction.

Reliability is defined as "The probability that a device will perform its intended function for a stated period of time under stated conditions". 95/95 (or XX/YY) confidence and reliability is appropriate when we are discussing lifetime of a product or performance over time. For single use devices, it is appropriate when referring to the probability that the device will properly perform its intended function when called upon to do so.

Confidence/Reliability is a misnomer when we are referring to the (XX) confidence that a particular lot of product has less than a (YY) certain level of nonconformities. The misuse of reliability in this context is not egregious, but can mislead people regarding what is meant by reliability or into thinking that reliability is truly being measured somehow when in reality we are only measuring conformance to specification. Confidence and conformance more accurately portray our true intent.

36. Designing Time Accelerated Tests

Executive summary:

Testing products to design life is often time and cost prohibitive. What company can afford to place hundreds or thousands of devices on test for years before bringing a product to market? The problem is exacerbated by the fact that, with reliability testing, companies are trying to find a low failure rate. Accelerated testing allows companies to obtain failure rate estimates in a much shorter time than the design life. The two primary types of acceleration are time acceleration and force acceleration. Time acceleration is the purpose of this paper.

The concept can be applied to manufacturing processes as well as product designs. Many manufacturing processes either include tools subject to wear or may actually cause damage to the parts being manufactured. The article from which this paper is adapted dealt specifically with ultrasonic damage to thin SST (stainless steel) parts. In that case, the reliability target to demonstrate was 0.9997 reliability with 90% confidence. Doing this without accelerated testing would require processing 7675 parts, without failure. Use of time acceleration allowed for providing the same confidence using only 40 parts left in the ultrasonic bath for 14x the normal 5-minute exposure. From a practical standpoint, I have near zero (subjective) confidence that any inspector can inspect 7675 parts without making a mistake, yet that would be required in the absence of accelerated testing. I do have confidence, however, that an inspector can thoroughly inspect 40 parts.

This paper generalizes the procedure used in [Becker] from one specific application to use in a variety of applications.

Terminology:

This paper assumes the reader is generally familiar with reliability terms and the Weibull distribution. Brief definitions are included here.

- Weibull distributions: A family of distributions used to model failure times for products.
- Weibull shape: A parameter of the Weibull distribution that determines the shape of the distribution, also called Weibull slope. The Greek letter beta is typically used to represent shape.
- Characteristic life: A parameter of the Weibull distribution. By definition, characteristic life is that time by which 63.2% of the product will have failed. The Greek letter eta is typically used to represent characteristic life.
- Duty cycle: The portion of time a device is in active or operational state.

Background:

Many products are used only intermittently or exposed to processing methods for a short period of time. In these instances, one can test to failure simply by extending or accelerating the period of time to which the products are exposed to the relevant forces. Examples:

- Residential washing machines are used for only a few hours a week. Reliability testing can be accelerated by setting up machines to run continuously.
- In the washing machine example, start/stop cycles might be a primary stressing factor. Again, time acceleration can be utilized by starting and stopping the machine hundreds of times in a day.
- Residential lawnmowers are used for only a few hours a week. Reliability testing can be accelerated by setting up lawnmowers to run continuously.
- Fragile parts that are cleaned ultrasonically are exposed to ultrasonics for a limited time. They can be left in the ultrasonic bath for longer periods of time to determine susceptibility to damage.

- Machine tools wear. They may be in actual part contact for only a few hours a day or a few hours a week. Tool wear can be accelerated on a test stand that provides more frequent part contact.

Testing to failure using normal forces at standard duty cycles is often time prohibitive. Consider:
- Products are designed to have high reliability, so the failure rate will be low.
- Processing methods are designed to manufacture parts without damage and with a minimum of wear, again resulting in a low failure rate.
- It is difficult to detect a low failure rate, requiring extended time and a large sample size.

Theory:

Time-to-failure (TTF) distributions are often skewed right, sometimes heavily. This means that the vast majority of products will survive much longer than the design life. A typical TTF distribution is shown in figure 36.1. As can be seen from the figure, to achieve 99% reliability after 5 years, many products will need to survive for more than 50 years. By definition, slightly less than 37% of the products will survive 50 years.

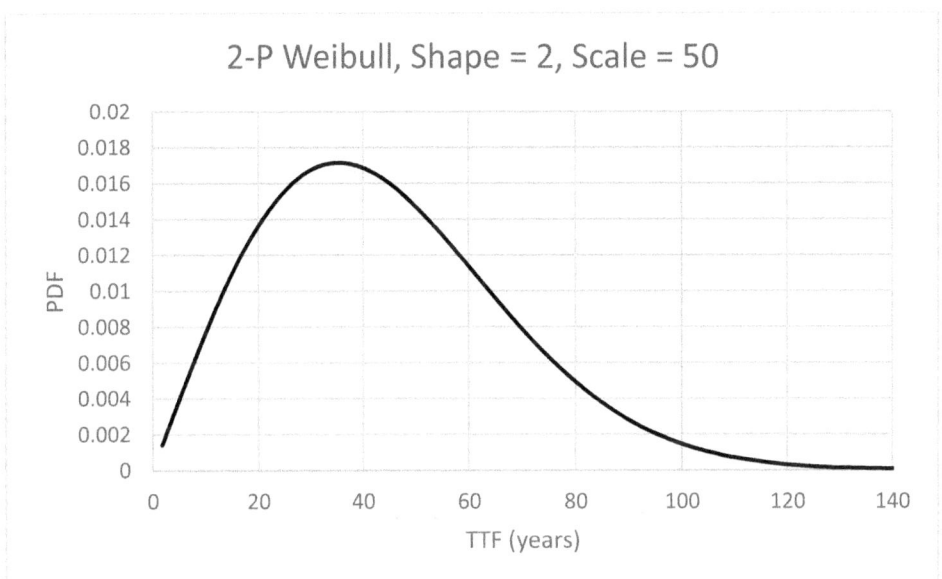

Figure 36.1 – PDF for R(5 years) = 0.99 with Weibull Shape = 2 and Scale (Characteristic Life) = 50

Standard, non-parametric life testing to demonstrate 0.90 (90%) reliability at 90% confidence with a zero failure test requires only 22 parts, although these parts still need to be tested for design life, 5 years for example. The sample size for this type of testing increases exponentially with increasing reliability as shown in figure 36.2.

169

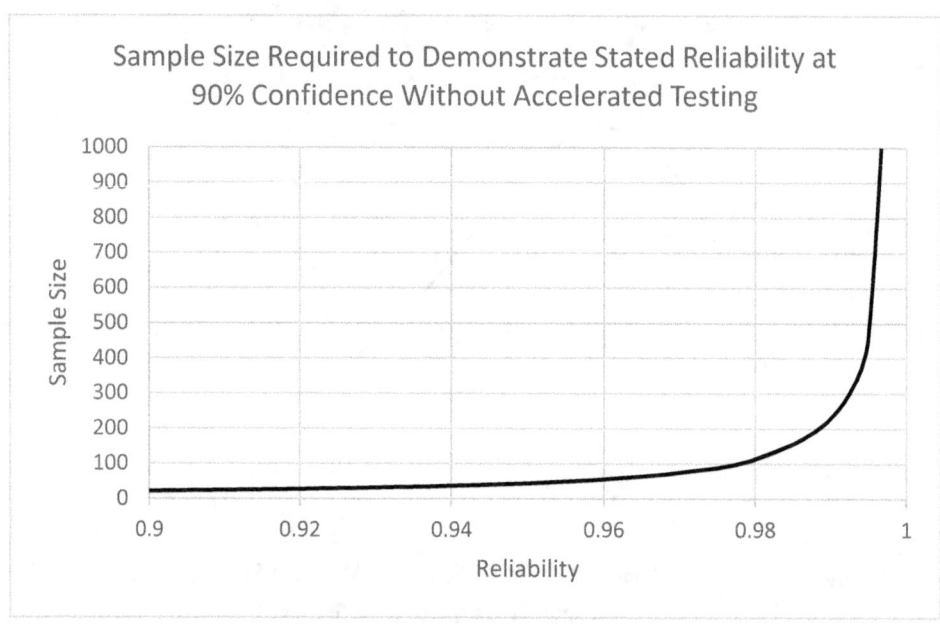

Figure 36.2 – Sample Size vs. Reliability, 90% Confidence, C=0 Testing, Without Acceleration

To achieve confidence that a reliability target has been met, we must test long enough to be have high confidence that, if the product fails to meet reliability targets, the test is almost certain to find failures. If we run such a test and do not find failures, we can then be confident that the reliability target has been met. If we test only to design life and the reliability target is close to 1, the sample size quickly becomes prohibitively large. However, figure 1 shows us that if we test for longer than the stated design life, we can expect to see failures with a smaller sample size. From figure 36.1, if we tested 20 years we would expect to see failures with a rather small sample size, but who can afford to test for 20 years? This is where time acceleration becomes useful. What if we can put the equivalent of 20 years' use on the devices in a matter of a few months? Now we can have an economically feasible test.

Procedure:

The general procedure for designing a time accelerated test is:
1. Determine:
    a. Reliability target
    b. Confidence level desired
    c. Forces expected to result in failure
    d. Intensity of those forces in the field or in the production process
    e. Duration of exposure to those forces experienced by the product (duty cycle)
2. Conduct testing to determine Weibull shape or use methods from the next paragraph.
3. Using this shape, calculate characteristic life to meet stated reliability goals.
4. Either choose a sample size and calculate the required test time OR choose a test time and calculate the required sample size to demonstrate the target has been met. This may be an iterative process.
5. Run the test and monitor for failures.
6. Analyze the results.
7. Improve the product or process and perform follow-up tests as necessary or appropriate.

One obvious question is "what if we don't know the Weibull shape and don't have adequate product to test to determine this?". A few options exist:
1. Use data from similar products to estimate Weibull shape if that data is available.
2. Search the literature for Weibull shape values for products with similar failure mechanisms.
3. A Weibull shape of 2.0 is a reasonably conservative starting estimate in the absence of any data. This estimate can be revised as test data becomes available.

a. The methods in this paper can be used to determine the risks inherent in using an incorrect estimate for Weibull shape.

The formula for determining required characteristic life is:

Eqn 36.1:

$$\eta = \frac{t_u}{[-\ln(R_u(t_u))]^{\frac{1}{\beta}}}$$

Where: $\eta = characteristic\ life$
$t_u = time\ exposed\ to\ the\ forces\ in\ the\ field\ (use)\ or\ in\ the\ process$
$R_u(t_u) = desired\ reliability\ at\ the\ stated\ use\ (or\ process)\ time$
$\beta = Weibull\ shape$

To determine sample size, given a stated test time first determine the reliability of the parts in the test, then calculate sample size for the stated test time. Equation 36.2 is used to calculate the expected reliability in the test, assuming the previously determined slope and characteristic life.

Eqn 36.2:

$$R_t(t_t) = e^{\left[-\left(\frac{t_t}{\eta}\right)^{\beta}\right]}$$

Where: $R_t(t_t) = reliability\ at\ end\ of\ test$
$t_t = test\ duration$
$e = base\ of\ natural\ logarithms$

Next, calculate sample size from:

Eqn 36.3:

$$n = \frac{ln[P(n)]}{ln[R_t(t_t)]}$$

Where: P(n) = (1 – desired confidence) expressed as a proportion.
$n = sample\ size$
Example: for 90% confidence, P(n) = 1 – 0.9 = 0.1.

To determine required test duration for a given sample size, we first calculate required reliability in the test using equation 36.4, then calculate test time via equation 36.5.

Eqn. 36.4:

$$R_t(t_t) = [P(n)]^{\frac{1}{n}}$$

Eqn. 36.5:

$$t_t = \eta\left[-ln[R_t(t_t)]\right]^{\frac{1}{\beta}}$$

For the interested reader, equation 36.2 is the standard Weibull reliability equation as found in any number of texts. Equations 36.1 and 36.5 are re-arrangements of equation 36.2. Equations 36.3 and 36.4 are rearrangements of:

$$P(n) = R^n$$

Where: P(n) is simply the probability of all parts surviving the test (which as stated above is the complement of the desired confidence level). Given independence among the test units, the probability of all surviving is simply the product of the probability of each individual unit surviving. Given identical test units, this is simply the reliability of each unit on test raised to the power of the number of units on test.

173

Example 36.1:

Step 1: Reliability target is: R(2) = 0.995
Desired confidence is 90%
Force expected to cause failure is ultrasonic exposure
Intensity of force = 72 kHz, 1000W in a tank of stated geometry and loading
Duration of exposure = 2 minutes per part (hence R(2))

Note: this is stated as reliability in a manufacturing process, but could as easily be field reliability of a product for example if we simply change the force to a bending force of 4kN applied for a total of 560 hours over a span of 2 years. In such a case we may choose to change unit of measure from 2 years to 560 hours. The formulae will work as long as we keep the same unit of measure throughout once we have started.

Note: unaccelerated testing for this example would require a sample size of 460, C=0

Step 2: Weibull shape = 2.3 based on previous testing on a similar part.

Step 3: Using equation 36.1,

$$\eta = \frac{2}{[-\ln{(0.995)}]^{\frac{1}{2.3}}} = \frac{2}{0.005013^{0.43478}} = \frac{2}{0.100011} = 20.0$$

Characteristic life in the actual ultrasonic process needs to be 20 minutes to meet the stated requirements.

Step 4: Assume a desired test time of 10 minutes. From equation 36.2,

$$R = e^{\left[-\left(\frac{10}{20}\right)^{2.3}\right]} = e^{[-(0.5^{2.3})]} = e^{-0.20306} = 0.8162$$

Reliability in the test is estimated as 0.8162.

From equation 36.3,

$$n = \frac{\ln (0.1)}{\ln (0.8162)} = \frac{-2.30259}{-0.2031} = 11.3$$

We need a sample of 12 parts for a proper zero failure accelerated test design with the stated assumptions/requirements.

This same test design can be created in Minitab as follows.

From the menu, choose STAT\Reliability\Survival\Test Plans\Demonstration.

Per the assumptions/data in example 1, the dialog box should be filled out as in Figure 36.3.

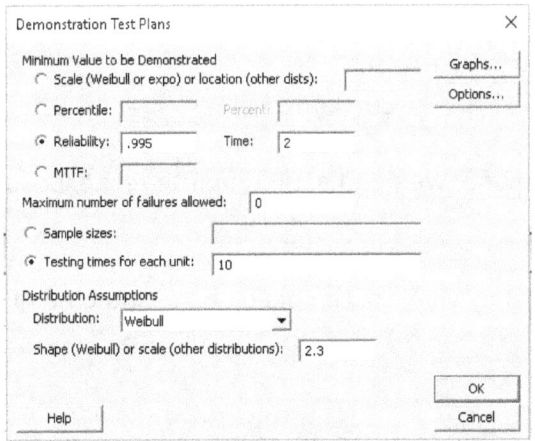

Figure 36.3 – Minitab dialog box for example 1

Figure 36.4 shows that the Minitab analysis results in the same sample size of 12 as calculated above.

Demonstration Test Plans

```
Reliability Test Plan
Distribution: Weibull, Shape = 2.3
Reliability Goal = 0.995, Target Confidence Level = 90%


                            Actual
Failure  Testing  Sample  Confidence
  Test     Time     Size     Level
    0       10       12     91.2585
```

Figure 36.4 – Minitab results for example 1

Assume the parts are expensive and we are only allowed 5 to test. From equation 36.4,

$$R = 0.1^{\frac{1}{5}} = 0.1^{0.2} = 0.631$$

Required test reliability is 0.631.

Using equation 36.5,

$$t = 20[-\ln{(0.631)}]^{\frac{1}{2.3}} = 20[0.46045]^{0.43478} = 14.28$$

For a sample size of 5, we need a 14.3 minute test exposure to ultrasonics.

To design this test in Minitab, the dialog box should be filled out as in figure 36.5.

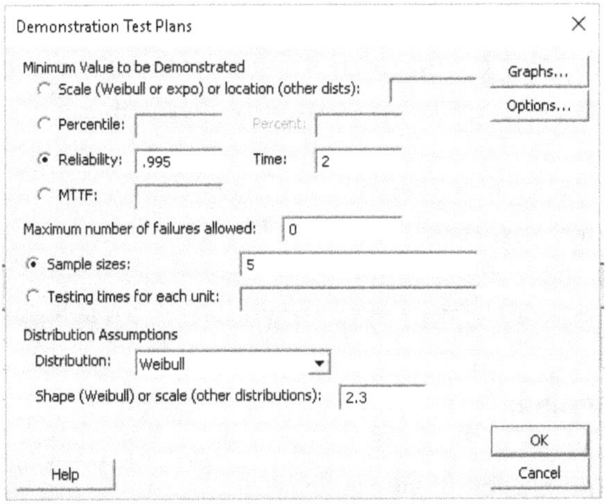

Figure 36.5 – Minitab dialog box for example 2

Figure 36.6 shows that the Minitab analysis results in the same (rounded) test time of 14.3 minutes.

```
Demonstration Test Plans

Reliability Test Plan
Distribution: Weibull, Shape = 2.3
Reliability Goal = 0.995,  Actual Confidence Level = 90%


Failure  Sample  Testing
 Test     Size    Time
   0        5    14.2755
```

Figure 36.6 – Minitab results for example 2

As shown, test time and sample size are mathematically related. We can select either and calculate the other and we can make tradeoff decisions – increase test time to reduce sample size or increase sample size to reduce test time.

Interpreting results:

It is a good practice to include justification for why the chosen slope is believed correct or reasonable.

It is also good practice to report confidence intervals around any estimates to avoid the appearance of unrealistic precision.

Three types of results can occur:
1. No failures observed
2. Failures observed within design life
3. Failures observed, but only after a test time exceeding design life

No failures observed:

If confident in the choice of Weibull slope, we may state that the reliability goal has been met, with the stated confidence.

If we are not confident in the Weibull slope, there are a few options:
1. Preface any statement with "If the assumed Weibull slope is correct. . ."
2. Run tests covering a range of plausible Weibull slopes. Only 2 tests at the extremes of the plausible Weibull slope range need be run.
   a. If both tests pass, we can be confident that the reliability target has been met.
   b. If both tests fail, we can be confident that the reliability target has not been met.
   c. If one test passes and the other fails, more testing and/or analysis is required.

Failures observed within design life:

If failures are observed within the design life, the reliability target has not been met and product or process improvements are required.

Failures observed only after test time exceeds design life:

178

In this situation, more testing is typically required. Multiple scenarios are possible.

1. High reliability at design life, but not high enough to meet targets. This would require product/process improvements.
2. Sufficiently high reliability at design life with a different Weibull slope than assumed, resulting in test failures. This would represent a product/process meeting design life and would require an estimate of Weibull shape different from original assumptions.
3. Failure-free time corresponding to a 3-parameter Weibull (not discussed further in this chapter).
4. A distribution other than Weibull is more suited to the situation at hand. This might indicate a product/process meeting the reliability targets or one failing to meet reliability targets.

Empirical results:

As detailed in [Becker], this technique was used to provide early indication of 3 failure modes that were occurring in production, either in our process or our customer's process (they also used ultrasonics), but had not been identified prior to this test. After finding these failure modes in the test, detailed investigation found them also happening in production.

The test was designed as part of new process development. The test identified 5 failure modes that were prevented with design changes, to either product or process, before the new process was implemented, thereby avoiding failures at the customer or in the field.

The test method exhibited a low false alarm rate, with zero of the failure modes being identified as a false alarm. That is, the predicted failure modes either occurred during actual design life or were designed out prior to the process being implemented. It is of course possible that one or more of the failure modes that were prevented in the process design

179

phase could have been a false alarm. However, the preventive solutions required less time and effort than the additional testing that would have been required to definitively determine whether any failure modes were false alarms.

A similar test was used for a different problem at the same employer. R = 0.9991 was predicted. We had the luxury of data in this case – 100% automated inspection with a run rate of hundreds of thousands of parts per week. This 100% inspection confirmed a reliability of R = 0.9992.

Closing remarks:

The procedure has been successfully used by this employer for years to test changes to product and process design, identifying risks in time to take preventive action before failures were experienced at customers.

Caution: this testing regime is designed as a zero failure test and as such does not provide adequate data to make detailed reliability estimates – it can only determine a lower bound for reliability under certain assumptions as detailed earlier. However, determination of the lower bound for reliability is often the central question to answer and the test readily provides this answer, thereby providing useful guidance for decision-making.

37. The Great Unsolved Quality Problem of Our Time

How should a company allocate scarce resources to preventive activities?

It is impossible to know apriori if, in the absence of preventive activities, certain negative consequences would occur. Much of engineering deals with the prevention of failure; many techniques such as FMEA, FTA, risk assessment, among others, deal with the prediction, and subsequent prevention, of failure.

There are two key aspects that make this the great unsolved quality problem of our time.
1. The consequences of failure to take preventive action may not be known for a long period of time, even years in the case of reliability failures.
2. The cost, even the occurrence, of those failures cannot be predicted with certainty until after they occur. If we can't predict the cost until after the event occurs, how do we justify allocating "X" dollars to prevention and how do we determine how large "X" should be?

If negative consequences do occur as a result of failing to take preventive action, it's impossible in advance to know the severity. If a product fails in the field, is it an annoyance to the user or does it result in serious injury or possibly death? We try to predict the outcome so we can make a correct decision, but until an event happens there is always uncertainty about that actual outcome. Let's take it out of the realm of injury. If a product is less reliable than desired, are the warranty claims reasonable or does it reach the level of a class-action lawsuit?

A GM once told me a story about a colleague who failed to speak up regarding a project likely to fail. That colleague ended up losing his job. This same GM, a few weeks later, became very upset with me **for** speaking up when I pointed out trends likely to create larger future problems. The GM stated I was being alarmist when I pointed out the potential problems and the message to me could easily be interpreted as 'it's better to keep quiet and be ready to pick up the pieces when things do fall apart rather than speak up and try to prevent a problem'. I wonder if the GM's former colleague had similar interactions that prevented him from pointing out the likely project failure.

In hindsight, many of the previous examples in this book should and could have been prevented given proper forethought. I would venture poor decisions were made by some pretty smart people, leading to serious financial losses and even complete business failures. How then does one go about planning for prevention?

If I had a complete answer, it wouldn't be the 'great unsolved quality problem'. Having said this, there are some relevant considerations.

Many outcomes are predictable via use of methods mentioned in this book and elsewhere.

- Proportion nonconforming in a lot of manufactured material can be predicted with reasonable precision via statistical sampling. One might argue truthfully that this is not preventive because the defects have already been manufactured. Alternatively, it could be argued this is preventive in the sense that the nonconformities have not yet been shipped to the customer.
- Looking back further into the process, an SPC chart can be used to identify a trend and fix a problem **before** any nonconforming product has actually been produced. This is truly preventive.
- Reliability and functional performance can be simulated by testing in the lab. This brings to mind one of my favorite quotes from George E.P. Box – *'all models are wrong, some models are useful'*. Lab testing attempts to simulate actual use but in reality is only an approximation. Still, lab testing provides essential data that can be used to predict future events. It's important to note that even though this data can predict the likelihood of a future event:
  - The specific consequences of that event remain uncertain.
  - The validity of the model is uncertain; it is, after all, wrong but hopefully useful.

The previous examples were data based. Let's move outside that realm.

- How much time should we invest in training? Training, if done properly is preventive. Once a person is fully trained, however, additional 'training' provides little if any value. How do we know when someone is fully trained?
  - o This applies across all industries. In the service industry, poor or rude service will drive away customers. Training can improve quality and courtesy of services, but how much is enough?
  - o Making this more difficult, the correct amount of training for one person will be inadequate for another and excessive for someone else.
- How much time should Management invest in reinforcing the idea of quality, be it quality of product or quality of service? This reinforcement is a preventive activity. In the absence of reinforcement, it's almost certain that quality will degrade (see 'thermodynamics in the workplace'), **but how much is enough**?
- Even the data-driven examples are subject to a very large uncertainty w.r.t. prevention – how many resources should be allocated to these preventive activities? If no engineers are assigned to perform FMEA, design and administer lab tests, analyze and report on the data, we will have no basis for predicting problems and acting to prevent them. Is one engineer enough, two, six, other? What factors need to be considered when making this decision?
- One of senior management's most difficult tasks is the determination of proper staffing levels. Staff too heavily and profitability suffers; staff too lightly and work is not accomplished and mistakes are made.
- [Deming, p. 20] states "The most important figures needed for management of any organization are unknown and unknowable." That concept certainly seems to apply here.
- [Deming, p. 107] illustrates a primary difficulty with preventive thinking another way "Heard in a seminar. One gets a good rating for fighting a fire. The result is visible; can be quantified. If you do it right the first time, you are invisible. You satisfied the requirements. That is your job. Mess it up, and correct it later, you become a hero."

183

So, how then does an individual contributor or a manager properly plan for prevention? This is a judgment call that requires both vision and courage. The importance of prevention varies by industry; plastic toys don't have the same risk profile as medical devices for example and the right answer for a toy factory CEO will be much different than the right answer for a medical device CEO. Furthermore, there is not one single, correct answer. Let's examine the resource question. The difference between management allocating 6 or 7 engineers to preventive activities may simply be a 17% (1/6 = 17% more resources allocated) difference in long-term costs that likely cannot be traced back directly to the staffing decision – or it may result in a failure that puts the company out of business. There is a mantra among reliability professionals that many companies don't get serious about reliability until they suffer an event (usually field failure) that threatens the existence of the company.

As an engineer:
- I would use my best judgment regarding preventive activities
- Gather whatever data were available
- Craft a reasonable argument regarding the 'unknown and unknowable' factors
- Make a recommendation to senior management

As a Manager/Director, I would often be in a position of having engineers or others present the information above, then make the required judgment call.

This topic would make for an interesting panel discussion at an industry conference.

38. Derivation for Attribute Sample Size Rule of Thumb

Applicability:

I learned of this rule of thumb (explicitly stated in the next section) in one of the University of Maryland Reliability Engineering courses. It seemed pretty straightforward. Like any rule of thumb it is subject to certain assumptions and works better when those assumptions are met. Since the instructor didn't list the limitations, the only way to understand the potential errors/risks of using the rule of thumb is to derive it ourselves. The stated rule of thumb is based on the binomial distribution and is applicable under the following conditions:

- Attribute sampling
- $C = 0$ sampling (i.e. reject on a single defect)
- Group of parts under consideration is homogeneous – that is, defects are randomly distributed throughout the group.
    - The chance of pulling a defective part depends only on p, the proportion defective.
- Proportion defective is low (below 0.1 or 10%).
- Samples are statistically independent.
    - Homogeneous group of parts as indicated above.
    - Calculated sample size is less than 5% of the total parts being sampled. Note: if sample size is much greater than 5% of the parts being sampled, hypergeometric equation should be used instead of binomial. This gets a little more complicated and a rule of thumb is not known, but the calculations are still manageable.

Rule of thumb:

For 95% confidence, select a sample size such that, if the defect rate is truly equal to the hypothesized defect rate p, the expected number of defects found in the sample is np = 3. If we then inspect the stated sample size and find zero defects, we can state with 95% confidence that the true defect rate is equal to or less than the hypothesized rate.

For 90% confidence, select a sample size such that, if the defect rate is truly equal to the hypothesized defect rate p, the expected number of defects, np = 2.3. Interpretation is analogous to the above except the confidence level is 90% instead of 95%.

Where: n = sample size
p = defect rate expressed as a proportion

A similar rule of thumb can be derived for any other desired confidence level following the method below.

Derivation:

For statistically independent samples:

$$P(X \cap Y) = P(X) * P(Y)$$

If proportion defective is p, the probability of pulling a good part in the sample is equal to (1-p) and the probability of pulling all good parts (i.e. no defects) is given by:

$$P_a = (1 - p)^n$$

Where: P_a = the probability of acceptance or the probability of pulling only good parts
p = proportion defective
n = sample size

If we set up the experiment such that P_a = 0.1 (10%) at the hypothesized proportion defective p and we fail to find any defects, we are 90% confident that the true proportion defective is less than p. Similarly, if we set up the experiment such that P_a = 0.05 (5%) at the hypothesized proportion defective p and we fail to find any defects, we are 95% confident that the true proportion defective is less than p.

The rule of thumb:

First, take natural logarithms of both sides of the previous equation:

$$P_a = (1 - p)^n$$

$$ln(P_a) = nln(1 - p)$$

Now we need to rely on the following approximation:

$$ln(1 - p) \approx -p$$

The wavy equal sign means approximately equal.

Substituting:

$$ln(P_a) = -np$$

$$n = -\frac{ln(P_a)}{p}$$

At 95% confidence, P_a = 0.05.

$$ln(0.05) = -np$$

$$-2.9957 = -np$$

$$3 \approx np$$

$$n \approx \frac{3}{p}$$

For 90% confidence, P_a = 0.1 and ln(0.1) = -2.3026. Therefore for 90% confidence:

$$np \approx 2.3$$

$$n \approx \frac{2.3}{p}$$

A similar rule of thumb can be created for any confidence level desired.

The table below provides selected values of p and ln(1-p) to demonstrate that the approximation is appropriate for low proportion defective. The table goes beyond 0.1 to illustrate how quickly (or slowly) error in the approximation increases.

-p	ln(1-p)	% Error
-0.0001	-0.000100005	-0.005%
-0.001	-0.0010005	-0.05%
-0.005	-0.005012542	-0.25%
-0.01	-0.010050336	-0.5%
-0.05	-0.051293294	-2.52%
-0.1	-0.105360516	-5.09%
-0.15	-0.0162518929	-7.7%
-0.25	-0.287682072	-13.1%
-0.5	-0.693147181	-27.87%

Examples: How many parts need to be inspected using a C = 0 plan to demonstrate with 90% confidence that the defect rate is less than 0.2% (2000 DPPM)?

$$n = \frac{2.3}{0.002} = 1150$$

95% confidence?

$$n = \frac{3}{0.002} = 1500$$

How many parts need to be inspected using a C = 0 plan to demonstrate with 90% confidence that the defect rate is less than 0.03% (300 DPPM)?

$$n = \frac{2.3}{0.0003} = 7667$$

95%?

$$n = \frac{3}{0.0003} = 10,000$$

You may recognize that in the chapter re: Designing Time Accelerated Tests, we calculated a sample size of 7675 for 90% confidence of 300 DPPM (presented there as a reliability of 0.9997). The rule of thumb only differs from the exact calculation by 0.1%.

39 Effect of Measurement Error on Process Capability

A common rule of thumb in industry related to measurement error is:
- Less than 10% of tolerance is desirable
- Less than 20% of tolerance is acceptable
- Less than 30% of tolerance is acceptable with justification

In practice, less than 30% often becomes the default for acceptance.

Wait, we can really give up almost a third of the tolerance to measurement error? This is a surprise to many. What they're missing are the implications of the root-sum-of-squares (RSS) manner in which measurement error contributes to overall process capability. Crudely stated, with RSS, the major contributor to variation often dominates the other contributors.

Let's use an example to illustrate.

Given:
Cpk = 1.1
10% GR&R using 6 sigma measurement error
Tolerance = 50 +/- 1
Process is perfectly mean centered

Find: Cpk if measurement error increases to 30% of tolerance

Equation 1 illustrates mathematically how measurement error contributes to overall error (error given in terms of standard deviation or sigma, remembering that standard deviation is simply the square root of the variance)

$$\sigma_{tot}^2 = \sigma_{prod}^2 + \sigma_{meas}^2 \qquad \text{eqn 1}$$

σ_{tot}^2 represents total variation (variance) which is a combination of product variation and measurement variation.

σ_{prod}^2 represents variation (variance) of the product **without** measurement error. It's important to understand that we can never directly determine this value.

190

Since we can only obtain a value for any dimension by measuring it, measurement error is completely confounded with product variation for any real data.

σ^2_{meas} represents measurement error (variance)

While we cannot directly determine product variation independently of measurement error, methods to directly determine measurement error have been developed and are commonly known. Of course, the collected measurements allow us to directly calculate overall variation. Once measurement error and overall variation have been determined, we can calculate product variation by a simple rearrangement of equation 1.

Measurement (msmt) error at 10%:
6s msmt = 0.2 (10% of tolerance range of 2)
1s msmt = 0.033333

$$Cpk = \frac{USL - \bar{\bar{x}}}{3s} \qquad \text{eqn 2}$$

Rearranging and solving equation 2, 1s total = 0.303

Rearranging equation 1 and solving for 1s product gives us:

$$\sigma_{prod} = \sqrt{0.303^2 - 0.03333^2} = 0.301$$

This result already provides insight into the RSS effect. While measurement error is 10% of overall tolerance, 1s total is less than 1% larger than 1s product ((0.303-0.301)/0.303).

If msmt error increases to 30%, 1s total increases to:

6s msmt = 0.6, 1s msmt = 0.1

$$\sigma_{tot} = \sqrt{0.301^2 + 0.1^2} = 0.317$$

$$Cpk = \frac{1}{3(0.317)} = 1.05$$

Conclusion: increasing measurement error from 10% to 30% in this example only decreases Cpk from 1.1 to 1.05, a 4.5% decrease. The actual value of a 4.5% decrease in Cpk is specific to this example. The general analysis method can be used for other situations.

40. Short Bites

Thermodynamics (entropy) in the workplace:

My college thermodynamics professor had a great way of explaining entropy. He held a ceramic coffee mug and said if he dropped the mug it would break into a thousand pieces; those thousand pieces would never spontaneously assemble into a coffee mug. Briefly, the concept of entropy states that, in the absence of work, the universe tends toward disorder or chaos; conversely, work is required to create order out of disorder.

In the workplace, and particularly with respect to quality, a company's QMS will slowly fall apart unless constant effort is applied to keep it functioning effectively. How can this happen?
- Post-It notes slowly make their way into the manufacturing area in place of approved Work Instructions.
- Employees start following verbal instructions rather than approved Work Instructions.
- Hotel rooms are not cleaned and prepped as well as they used to be.
- Some of the checklist items during routine vehicle maintenance are not consistently performed.
- Equipment maintenance is not performed to the same degree.
- Shortcuts happen during the training process.
- FMEAs become a check-the-box exercise.
- Document reviews turn into pencil whipping.
- Etc., etc., etc. – the examples continue ad infinitum.

Conditions of rapid growth place much more strain on the QMS, tend to hasten the effects of entropy, and require considerably more effort to maintain the health of the Quality Management System.

How does one prevent this deterioration? Many methods exist including:

- QMS audits
- Management review
- Daily reinforcement of QMS principles by management from senior to line level
- Continually improving the QMS.
- Watching for, and taking action to prevent, normalization of deviance.
- Responding promptly and properly to concerns brought up by production employees.
- Explaining the rationale (why) behind QMS decisions to all employees, not only to management.
- A review of industry standards such as ISO 13485 will illustrate many of these methods.

Million dollar question:

A customer had rejected product for many months; they measured the parts out of tolerance; we measured them in tolerance. The dollar value of product rejected by the customer eventually exceeded $1M. To make this more difficult, the dimension being measured used custom measuring fixtures that could not be directly calibrated to NIST standards. To be clear, we could calibrate the loadcell traceable to NIST, but the measurement in question was highly dependent on how the part was held while being presented to the loadcell; this fixturing could not be calibrated to a NIST traceable standard.

My manager at the time called me into his office, looked me straight in the eye, and asked if I was certain that we were right on this issue. I understood the implications of the question – should we accept the $1M return of product? After considering multiple factors, I was able to reply that, yes, we took all of the proper precautions and I was confident the parts met tolerance.

Months later, the SQE (Supplier Quality Engineering) manager from the customer was visiting and asked to speak to me outside. He proceeded to tell me that they found a problem with their measurement fixtures and, in fact, we were correct all along. The customer never formally admitted the mistake, only this off-the-record conversation, but they did accept all of the product that had been previously rejected. (This happened to be the same manager referenced in the 'most interesting customer audit' and, temporally, occurred prior to the audit).

Most difficult decision:

Personnel decisions regarding discipline or layoffs have always been difficult for me. Who am I to decide someone else's future? That said, I've had to make many such decisions; they're always difficult. This book, however, is not about those types of decisions. Focusing on technical/business decisions, it's tough to select one, but the following ranks at or near the top in difficulty. The next example expands upon one first mentioned in Chapter 5 – Worst Possible Answer.

I received a phone call on the weekend while working as a Quality Engineer. The call related to the same measurement fixtures used in the 'million-dollar question' story above. The parts being measured were easily damaged in a way that would lead to wrong, but believable measurements and the fixtures would sometimes measure incorrectly. Because of this we had 10-12 "standard" parts with known values that were used to monitor the fixtures and determine whether they were measuring properly.

195

Typically, one of two issues occurred. Either one or a few standard parts were damaged or one or a few measurement fixtures would start measuring incorrectly. In the former instance we could identify the bad parts based on the majority that had not changed. The bad parts would then be replaced with new standard parts. In the latter, all standard parts would provide similar values and only one or a few measurement fixtures out of dozens would be measuring incorrectly.

This particular weekend, all of the standard parts consistently indicated that all of the measuring fixtures were measuring wrong, by roughly the same amount, in roughly the same direction.

It was highly unlikely that all of the standard parts would be damaged by the same amount, the same direction, at the same time. Furthermore, it was highly unlikely that all measurement fixtures would change by the same amount at the same time. In fact, neither of these events had occurred previously, and neither have occurred since. To make things even more confusing, we had a second set of 10-12 standard parts as a backup. These backup parts were stored in a different location and never used, the theory being if something happened to damage all of the standard parts at the same time, the backups could be used. *These backup standards also indicated that all measurement fixtures changed by roughly the same amount as the primary standards.*

At the time, we were severely capacity constrained; our customers wanted much more product than we were able to deliver. We did have another manufacturing facility, making the same type of product, approximately 4 hours away by car.

I had to decide whether to shut down manufacturing because the measurement fixtures had all moved or to run at risk until we could resolve the issue. Running at risk could easily result in a 6 or 7-figure scrap cost and shutting down would result in unrecoverable manufacturing delays. How does one decide the best course of action when faced with two highly unlikely events? The decision really came down to two factors. First, I believed it less likely that all fixtures would change by the same amount at the same time than all 24 standard parts changing by the same amount. Second, because we were already capacity constrained, shutting down the process would have caused lost production that could never be recovered. In the end, the decision was made more on business impacts than on science; I had no good way to assign probabilities to either of the highly unlikely events mentioned above.

Decision: continue to run at risk and have new standard parts shipped from the other manufacturing facility.

Result: the standard parts from the other facility confirmed that our fixtures were measuring correctly and all our parts were acceptable. We never determined what event led to the highly unlikely outcome of all primary and backup standard parts changing in the same direction by approximately the same amount. The situation never arose again.

Statistics work even when the answer is not obvious:

We had two similar product lines for which I was responsible. The customer was complaining about contamination on one line, but not the other. The difference in contamination rate on the manufacturing lines was only 0.5%, yet statistically significant since the quantities were large. I led a team to reduce the higher contamination rate and eliminate/reduce the corresponding customer complaints. The team consisting of engineers and a production lead worked on the problem for months without resolution and was disbanded. A few weeks after disbanding, I received a call from the lead saying she had found the problem.

The parts were manufactured 12 parts on a carrier strip. The product line with low contamination had a custom tool to remove rejects while on the product line with high contamination, defective parts were removed by manually bending the defective part until it broke off the strip. It was discovered that the manual removal resulted in transfer of contamination to the adjacent part even though the operators were wearing finger cots/gloves. This discovery led to the creation of a tool for removing defective parts on the product with a higher contamination level and the problem went away. People on the team were disbelieving that the difference in contamination levels between the two products was actually real because we couldn't find the cause; we just hadn't yet looked in the right location.

Rigid rules loosely enforced or loose rules rigidly enforced?

I've been involved in this philosophical discussion many times and have a clear preference for loose rules rigidly enforced. By loose rules, I don't mean allowing violation of requirements, rather that the rules enforce the requirements but don't go beyond those requirements.

The reason is simple; whenever rules are loosely enforced, nobody really knows which rules matter. Even worse, the rules that are enforced change from one day to the next depending on the situation or who specifically is making the decision. In such an environment, all blame should fall to Management, not the individuals doing the work.

Ask the person doing the work:

This has been stated so often, I don't remember where I first heard it, but I observed an almost perfect example of it in action. While participating in an FMEA, multiple times during the discussion the Engineer would assert "this is what happens. . ." only to have the Manufacturing lead say "no, this is what we really do". I might have laughed out loud, but if not was definitely laughing internally. One couldn't make up a better

198

example to illustrate the concept. Had the lead not had been part of the process, the FMEA would have been based on misinformation and likely resulted in many hours of wasted effort fixing the wrong issues. The presence of the lead prevented the FMEA from becoming an interesting piece of fiction.

Most interesting interviews:

I had applied for a job and happened to be sitting next to the hiring manager when he called HR to instruct them to offer me the job. HR was telling him he needed to interview me. I heard the following (as I was laughing).
"I've worked with him for years and know he can do the job."
"I don't need to interview him."
"Ok, fine. Kevin, how are you doing?" (to which I answered 'fine' or something to that effect).
"There, I interviewed him, now offer him the job."

The other that comes to mind is me going into the VP of Quality's office and saying "I heard the company is considering a corporate reliability engineer job. I would be interested in that position." A few months later, I was told the job was available if I were still interested. It was never officially posted.

Most interesting customer audit:

The customer Auditor was new to the company and accompanied by his manager. I had worked with the manager for a number of years and we had a good working relationship; in fact it was the same SQE Manager involved in the million-dollar question. The Auditor started asking questions, his manager began answering for me. This continued through almost the entire audit; I spent more time being amused than actually answering questions.

199

Quotes on my board at work:

I've found over the years a number of quotes that are useful enough to have continually posted on my board at work. Some I can attribute, for others I don't know the source.

1. "Engineering is hard work. Get over it." (author unknown). I'm often surprised at how many engineers seem to think the whole reason for going to college is to get a piece of paper. Surprise, it's not; it's to learn ways of solving difficult problems. While teaching engineers, I will often remind them that they're paid to think not just to blindly follow the work of others. Of course, thinking requires us to consider how the work of others might apply to our current problem and how using it might result in a better or quicker solution.

2. "It ain't what you don't know that gets you into trouble. It's what you know for sure that just ain't so." (Mark Twain). I've argued this point with many engineers and managers over the years. It's common to think we know more than we really do. I was fortunate enough to experience a classic example. Engineers were convinced that a certain dimension was not critical to our customer because "we know that our customer's welding process will compensate for that dimension". The topic arose as a side issue during a different discussion with the customer and I learned that while the customer's process would indeed compensate for a limited amount of variation in the dimension, if that variation exceeded a certain amount, it could result in weld spatter causing an electrical short and failure of the device after implantation into someone's body. Thankfully, we did not take any (wrong) action based on the "knowledge" that the dimension didn't matter.

3. "All models are wrong, some models are useful." (George E.P. Box). I mention this quote in almost every class I teach. Much (most) of what we do as engineers involves modeling – sampling, DOE, FEA, lab testing, etc.
    a. Example: reliability testing in the lab is a model. The lab testing does not recreate the actual experience in use; it can't since every device will be used a little differently and it's impossible to know apriori all of the conditions to which a device will be exposed. It's likewise impossible to replicate in the lab every device ever built. The only real reliability data is field data, but field data takes too long to gather and is notoriously messy - repair folks may not always record all the evidence or use consistent language to describe the same condition.
    b. Example: sampling looks at some of the parts to draw a conclusion about all of the parts. Clearly, the sample is only an estimate, albeit an educated one.
    c. Typical accelerated aging at elevated temperature assumes an activation energy that, while hopefully close to reality, is almost certainly wrong for a given situation.
    d. The examples are numerous enough that maybe this should be a separate chapter. An engineer's job in a Manufacturing environment is to make decisions that help the company be successful. These decisions need to be made in a timely manner and be correct more often than not. Quick, accurate decisions of necessity rely on modeling the real situation. There is no other choice and understanding the uncertainties and risks involved in the model helps us make better decisions.
4. "The system needs to support the business, not the other way around." (original). There are many ways to be compliant with

regulations and industry standards. Only one of those possible ways will be most effective/efficient and best for the company. I've seen many compliant, elegant, yet very wasteful systems created. Some folks have difficulty grasping the concept in this quote. We had an audit finding for failure to follow our own procedure. I was in a room with a couple dozen engineers and the manager was describing the failure and how we could comply. One problem: while compliant with industry standard, the procedure was wrong for the company. After a short time listening in disbelief to the discussion, I asked why we weren't just changing the procedure to something that made sense. This felt like saying 'the Emperor has no clothes', but I couldn't stay silent any longer.

5. "If doing the right thing were always easy, it would always be the first choice." (original with a colleague, Tim Coughlin). This quote originated after another internal debate re: whether or not we needed to inform a customer about a situation (ref chapter 2 – Principle Based Business). The answer was clear, but it was difficult. The difficulty led to debate. If the required action were easy, there would have been no debate.

6. "Trust is like a tree. It takes a long time to grow, but only a moment to cut down." (original). This quote is also mentioned in chapter 4 – Maintaining Credibility. I've pointed to this quote many times in discussions with others, even being so direct as to say "you realize your actions were chopping at that tree".

Why is changing manufacturing facility a big deal?

Changing manufacturing facility entails a lot of work – revalidation, audits, etc. and people often question the value of this work. After all, we're building the same product using the same or equivalent equipment and following the same procedures; what's the big deal?

A corporate value at one company where I worked stated "people are the source of our strength". The new facility was an expansion and would be hiring all new people. A manager was arguing that the change was low risk and we could significantly reduce the validation activities. I finally asked the manager if we truly believe our values. If it's true that people are the source of our strength and the new facility will have over 90% new employees (some employees were moving), how can we possibly view the new facility as low risk?

New management = different culture, even with the same procedures.

New facility = new layout. Currently, employees choose the correct location by rote. Does the new facility even yet have a location designated for discrepant material? Certainly, the location is not identical. Does the new facility have identical contamination controls? Probably not and definitely not in the same location within the building.

New employees = new habits. Even with a good QMS, much of what is done is due to tribal knowledge (i.e. information passed on from person-to-person, often not in writing); procedures cannot describe every nuance and detail.

Moving equipment, or buying new, is a large job. I've never seen a company staff appropriately for this. Those responsible for executing are typically overworked and prone, even encouraged, to take shortcuts.

Good engineering decisions:

It seems silly to even write this down, but given the number of times bad practices occur, it is evidently necessary. Good engineering decisions:

- Are based on data. Not everything is known or knowable as stated by Dr. Deming. However, a good engineer will strive to learn as much of what is knowable as feasible to make a sound decision.
- Are supported by objective evidence.
- Have a firm mathematical and/or scientific basis.
  - When theory and empirical testing agree, our confidence is greatest.
- Are subject to rigorous scrutiny.
  - Look for contrary evidence. Try to prove yourself wrong; examine the problem from different perspectives and solicit opinions from people who may not agree. When we honestly try to prove ourselves wrong and can't our confidence has improved dramatically.
  - Avoid confirmation bias (confirmation bias entails looking only for or only considering information supporting our pre-existing beliefs).

Good engineering decisions are **not**:
- Based on opinion in lieu of data/facts.
- Based on the loudest voice in the room or the most forceful personality.
- Lacking documented justification.
- Based on poor experimental design or analytical approach.
  - Failure to consider relevant factors.
  - Improper assumptions.
  - Failure to rigorously test hypotheses.

5 Distinct Categories – Always, Really?

[AIAG, p. 78] states that the number of distinct categories should be greater than 5. Customers have rejected GR&Rs failing to meet this criteria. In some cases, I agree. In others, it makes no sense. Consider the

204

process in figure 40.1. The specification limits are the vertical lines at the left and right edges of the graph. The process is so consistent that it would be common for a measurement system with less than 20% GR&R to have less than 5 distinct categories.

In this instance:
- Total standard deviation is 0.95
- 6 sigma = 5.7
- Tolerance range is 40
- 6 sigma total covers only 14% of the tolerance range. Since measurement error is an integral, inseparable part of every part measurement, GR&R cannot be more than 14% and, since the process has to induce some variation, is in reality less than that.

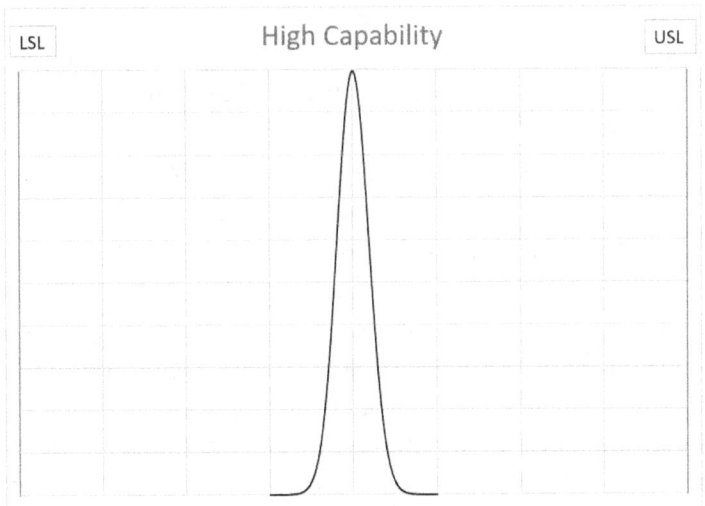

Figure 40.1 – High Capability Process

Process Ppk = 7.0 and most of us would agree that this is not only acceptable, but highly desired. Let's assume that measurement error makes up a large enough proportion of total variation such that we cannot distinguish 5 distinct categories.

The overall process, including measurement variation, is very capable, yet the measurement system fails. It doesn't make sense. How can this be? In a certain context it does make sense, in another not. [AIAG, p. 47] provides a little more insight; in Figure I-E.3 it explicitly states that if we have 5 or more distinct categories the measurement system may be used with variables control charts and **herein lies the distinction**.

For what purpose is the measurement system being used? If we want to use the measurement system for process improvement, i.e. with variables control charts, it needs to be able to distinguish parts within the process from each other and it makes sense that 5 distinct categories is an appropriate criteria. I ask, however, how many companies have so few problems that they will spend scarce resources to improve a process with a 7.0 Ppk. Every company I've worked with would seek only to maintain this process and to ensure that it does not shift to the point where we are in danger of nonconforming product. It would be common then to use the measurement system only for product acceptance. This measurement system, with guaranteed less than 14% GR&R, is plenty capable of distinguishing between a part from the distribution in figure 40.1 and a nonconforming part. Stated another way, if the measurement system is only to be used for acceptance sampling, the criterion of 5 distinct categories is spurious and unnecessary (5 distinct categories throughout the tolerance range would make sense, but the 5 distinct categories typically refer to the range of the data). Measurement equipment is expensive; how would you justify spending 6 or 7 figures on a new piece of measurement equipment for the process in figure 40.1? If you can, you should probably be in Sales as you could easily retire early from commissions. Still, some will blindly require the 5 distinct categories regardless of considerations such as those presented here.

41. Acceptance Sampling for a Highly Capable Process

Objective: Derive a sampling methodology allowing for smaller sample sizes than given in traditional sampling plans.

Background:
Acceptance Sampling is still widely used despite its predicted demise in the 80s. At its core, acceptance sampling provides assurance of a certain quality level.

Assurance statements of the form XX/YY will be used throughout. Often in the medical device industry, this is erroneously referred to as confidence and reliability. Reliability is, loosely, the probability of failure over time and with respect to acceptance sampling time is not a factor. Rather we are interested in the confidence that at least YY percentage (proportion) of the parts are conforming. Example: 95/99 refers to 95% confidence that at least 99% of the product is conforming. If our sampling plan has only a 5% chance of acceptance with a 1% nonconforming rate, and the sample passes, it can be said that we have 95% confidence (100 − 5) that the true nonconforming rate is less than 1% or, conversely, 95% confidence that at least 99% of the parts are conforming.

Loosely, for a given sampling plan, AQL is that quality level with a high probability of acceptance and LTPD is that quality level with a low probability of acceptance. In the examples below, 90/YY represents the LTPD and 10/YY represents the AQL (note: traditionally, AQL is stated as the quality level with a 0.95 probability of acceptance. 0.90 is used here because those values are tabulated in Squeglia). This might at first glance seem backward, but remember that confidence is (1 − probability of acceptance) and in OC curves the probability of acceptance is graphed against % nonconforming, **not** % conforming. We will continue with both sets of terminology: probability of acceptance vs. proportion or %

nonconforming, and confidence/conformance when drawing a connection between acceptance sampling and assurance level.

Examples from tables in [Squeglia] where C=0 in all instances:
- A 2.5 AQL with a lot size of 500 results in a sample size of 16.
  - There is a 0.10 (10%) probability of acceptance if the lot is 13.2% defective and a 0.90 probability of acceptance if the lot size is 0.64% defective.
    - This provides us with an assurance level of 90/87 or 10/99.4 (values rounded).
    - Following this general method, the assurance can be stated in the form of XX/YY for any desired nonconforming rate.
- A 0.65 AQL with a lot size of 1200 results in a sample size of 47.
  - This sampling plan provides us with a 90/95 or 10/99.8 assurance level.
- Note: in practice I've never seen confidence stated as low at 10% as in the examples here and would not recommend stating confidence levels below 80%. This notation is used simply to provide a link between XX/YY assurance and AQL/LTPD.
  - Confidence levels in common use are 90 and 95%. I've seen confidence levels range from 80 - 99%.

The above examples deal with attribute sampling. Variables sampling plans exist, allowing us to reduce the sample size. Still, for the sampling plans reviewed in [Taylor], 15 was the smallest sample size for variables sampling.

Key principle:

Traditional acceptance sampling relies on comparison to **specification limits**. With a highly capable process, we can set **action limits** much tighter than specification limits, thereby providing early warning of a change to the process and similar assurance levels with a much-reduced sample size.

Discussion:

This discussion assumes the reader is familiar with the following concepts/methods and able to use them effectively without detailed instructions:
- Ppk
- Z-values
- Z-tables
- Area under the curve

I've seen multiple processes with legitimate Ppk values in the range of 5 – 12. Some of these processes, like welding, can only be directly assessed via destructive testing that can become quite expensive. Even in the case of quick, inexpensive measurements, it borders on Quality malpractice to allow such a process to even approach the tolerance limit before taking action; yet this is exactly what traditional acceptance sampling does.

I referenced earlier the predicted demise of acceptance sampling. This prediction was predicated upon the use of SPC. To be clear, **I am a strong proponent of SPC** and believe it to be the preferred method of process control. SPC was explicitly created to notify us when a process has changed and would be extremely valuable in avoiding the malpractice mentioned above. That being said, this chapter is directed at acceptance sampling. The high capability acceptance sampling can easily be used to complement SPC.

General procedure for high capability sampling:
1. Determine that the process in question is stable with a high capability.

    a. SPC is the traditional method of determining process stability.
2. Set **action** limits to reflect the natural capability of the process.
    a. We will use 3 sigma action limits although the approach works with other values; the calculated minimum sample sizes just change.
3. If a sample exceeds the action limits, select a larger sample from the same job to gain more confidence/a better understanding whether the process actually changed, how much, and the risk of nonconforming product in the job being sampled.
    a. Use traditional acceptance sampling tables to select this larger sample.
4. If the larger sample indicates that the process **has not** changed significantly, accept the lot and resume high capability sampling.
5. If the larger sample indicates that the process **has** changed significantly, yet all parts are in tolerance:
    a. Accept the lot.
    b. Analyze the process to determine what has changed and, if possible, correct it to bring it back into the former state.
    c. If the process has moved, is stable, still high (albeit different) capability, and we decide not to return it to the previous state, the high capability sample sizes need to be recalculated.
6. If any parts are found out of tolerance, reject the lot, create a nonconformance, and correct the process prior to resuming production.

Three primary types of changes create a risk of nonconforming product while using the high capability sampling plan:
1. A shift in mean
2. An increase in standard deviation
3. A change in distribution
    a. Example: from a normal to Weibull distribution.

The first two are directly examined in this paper. Short of a fundamental change to one of the process KPIVs (Key Process Input Variables), a change to the underlying distribution seems unlikely. Analyzing this third type of change is the subject for a future analysis. **The underlying assumption is that the process output is normally distributed and remains normally distributed. It may change in location (mean) and width (standard deviation) as long as it remains normally distributed.**

There is a fourth risk to consider: outliers from the distribution may be caused by handling or, in the case of welding, by a contaminant causing a burn-through for example. It is assumed in this chapter that outliers of this sort can be determined visually and the visual acceptance sampling is still performed using traditional methods.

A 95/95 assurance level is common in the medical device industry and will be used in the remainder of this chapter. The attribute sample size for this assurance level is 59 and variable sample size from [Taylor] is 15 or greater. Remember that the sample sizes in this paragraph assume we are comparing only to the specification limits.

Example 41.1 - Mean Shift:

Consider the process represented in figure 41.1. Fonts will be difficult to read on mobile media, so legends have been removed and relevant descriptions are included here.

- Tolerance is 100 +/- 20, so the left and right edges of the graph represent tolerance limits. They are not explicitly labeled to avoid clutter.
- The original distribution is between the two vertical lines labeled "action limits"
- The shifted distribution is outside the action limits.
- Original distribution relevant statistics:
  - Mean = 100

- o   Standard deviation = 0.95 (rounded)
- o   Ppk = 7
- Shifted distribution relevant statistics:
  - o   Mean = 94
  - o   Standard deviation = 0.95 (rounded)
  - o   Ppk = 4.9

Setting action limits as in 2a above, our action limits are at 97.1 and 102.9. How many samples do we need to determine whether or not the process has shifted from a mean of 100 (original location) to a mean of 94? A single sample will suffice. The probability of pulling a single sample from the shifted distribution that is between the action limits is less than 0.001. That is, we are greater than 99.9% certain to identify such a mean shift in a single sample. It's obvious from the graph that the shifted distribution greatly exceeds 95% conformance; one could say it is 100% conforming for all practical purposes. In this example, a single sample provides greater than 99.9/99.9 assurance, far exceeding our goal. If the mean were to shift far enough for 5% nonconforming (95% conforming), the probability of identifying such a shift in a single sample is obviously much higher than in the example shown. The example of a shifted mean is almost trivial, but was shown for completeness.

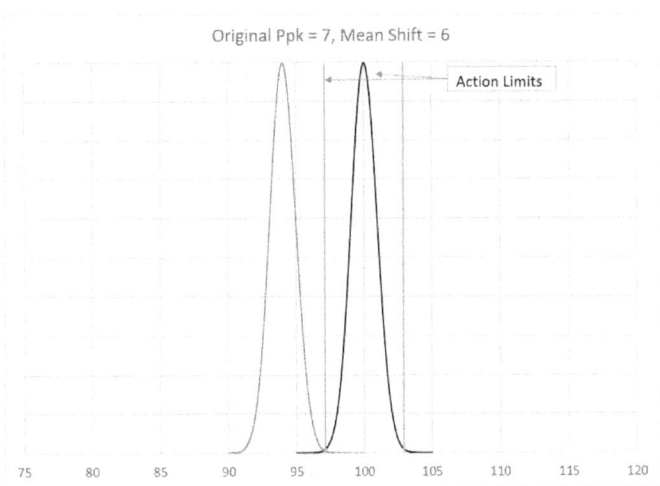

Original Ppk = 7, Mean Shift = 6

Action Limits

Figure 41.1 – Mean Shift

Of much more interest is a change in standard deviation. We need to recognize that there are an infinite number of normal distributions that would contain 95% conforming/5% nonconforming, three of which are shown in figure 41.2. For clarity, this figure again has the legend removed. As before, LSL and USL refer to Lower Specification Limit and Upper Specification Limit respectively. LAL and UAL refer to Lower Action Limit and Upper Action Limit respectively.

213

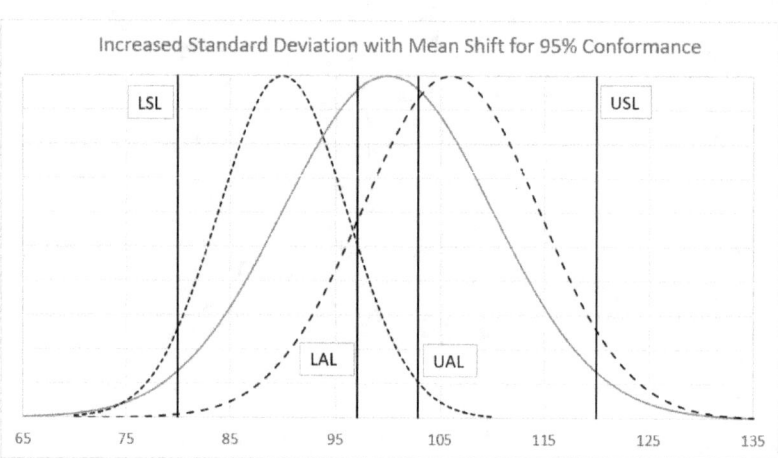

Figure 41.2 – Increased standard deviation plus mean shift to equal 95% conformance

Fortunately, we do not need to analyze hundreds or thousands of distributions; neither do we need techniques such as Monte Carlo Simulation, for one of these distributions represents worst case. Astute readers will be able to identify this worst case visually but since this is central to the analysis, a more formal demonstration is provided.

Our sampling objective is to identify, with 95% confidence, any change to the distribution resulting in 5% or more nonconforming. When we have such a change to the distribution, we need to select enough samples such that, with 95% confidence, at least one of the samples will fall **outside** the action limits. The probability of selecting a sample that falls **between** the action limits is given by the area of the curve between the action limits. The worst-case distribution is the one with the heaviest mass (largest area under the curve) between the action limits. Looking again at figure 41.2, it's easy to see that distribution 1, represented by the solid line, is worst case as it contains the largest area between the action limits. In general, the worst case distribution for our purposes is one that is centered around nominal with standard deviation increased to result in

95% conforming (5% nonconforming). This distribution has the highest probability of choosing a random sampling falling between the action limits and thus failing to identify that the distribution has changed and, as a result, will require the largest sample size to provide the stated assurance level.

The probability of accepting the entire sample is the probability that each part selected for measurement is between the action limits and is given by the equation below.

$$P_a = (1 - p)^n$$

P_a = The probability of accepting the entire sample
p = The probability of selecting an individual part that measures between the action limits. This is determined from a z-table
n = The number of parts in the entire sample

Solving for n:

$$n = \frac{ln(P_a)}{\ln (1 - p)}$$

For reference, relevant statistics for the distributions in figure 41.2 are below.

Distribution 1 (solid line centered between specification and action limits):
Mean = 100
Standard deviation = 10

Distribution 2 (left-most distribution):
Mean = 90
Standard deviation = 6.079

Distribution 3 (right-most distribution):
Mean = 106
Standard deviation = 8.51

Since distribution 1 is worst case, we will only determine required sample size for this one. The probability of randomly selecting a part to measure that falls between the action limits is, from z-tables, 0.2282. With this distribution we can, with 95% confidence, determine that the distribution has changed to an unacceptable state with as few as 3 samples. The calculation results in 2.03; convention is to round up the sample size to be conservative.

$$n = \frac{\ln{(0.05)}}{\ln{(0.2282)}} = \frac{-2.9957}{-1.4775} = 2.03$$

If this derivation is somewhat esoteric, a way to double check is to verify that there is less than a 0.05 probability (5% chance) of randomly selecting 3 consecutive samples from between the action limits. Assuming independence, the probability of all 3 samples falling between the action limits is 0.2282*0.2282*0.2282 = 0.012.

It should be disclosed that some rounding was used in this analysis. For example, +/- 2 standard deviations was taken to represent 95% of the distribution; more precisely this should be +/- 1.96 standard deviations.

Ideally, we would use SPC to control the process. Even if relying on acceptance sampling and using the methods in this paper, we would preferably plot the samples on a control chart to identify possible trends before they would become apparent given the small sample sizes.

False rejects

Our analysis would not be complete without considering the possibility of false failures. False failure is defined as concluding that the distribution has changed even though it hasn't.

Clearly, the likelihood of a false failure increases as the sample size increases. Since our action limits were set at +/- 3 standard deviations, there is a probability of 0.0027 that we will randomly find a part outside the action limits even when the distribution has not changed. With a 3-piece sample, this becomes 0.00808 (this is slightly less than 3*0.0027, the reason why is left to the reader).

Less than a 1/100 chance of a false failure is reasonable in many instances. We can increase or decrease the chance of a false failure by setting the action limits at other than +/- 3s. Doing so will, of course, affect the required sample size. It is worth noting that even if we had a false failure, the only cost is that of pulling a larger sample to better understand the situation.

This general method can be used for a wide range of capability values and XX/YY assurance levels. The lower the capability, the higher the required sample size and the higher the sensitivity to a slight departure from normality. This higher sensitivity requires increased analytical rigor to confirm normality and potentially larger than calculated sample sizes to compensate. Similarly, higher assurance levels will drive larger sample sizes. While the statistics here don't apply to non-normal distributions, the general methodology can, given proper modifications to account for the distribution being used.

I am not necessarily promoting 1-pc sample sizes, rather the concept that we can significantly reduce sample sizes if we're willing to set limits tighter than the tolerance limits, based on the process itself. Reduced sampling along these lines should be customized to the situation by a competent QE working with a competent Mfg Engineer. Examples:

- It would seem prudent, if a 1-pc sample is statistically justified, to measure 1 piece at the beginning of a job and a second at the end, both being compared to the tighter action limits. Why? This would provide assurance that the process started and ended in the expected location, or at least in an acceptable location. For this purpose, a random sample would be much less useful.
- Measuring 2 pieces instead of 1 provides at least some indication of process variation.

Conclusions:

1. Traditional acceptance sampling compares the measured values to the tolerance limits.
2. A high capability process has enough margin to the tolerance limits to allow for significantly smaller sample sizes **iff** (if and only if):
    a. The process is stable.
    b. The measured values are compared to action limits set to reflect the natural capability of the process rather than the tolerance limits.
    c. The sample size is calculated to provide the desired assurance level (XX/YY).

References:

- AIAG, Measurement Systems Analysis Reference Manual, Fourth Edition, 2010, Chrysler Group LLC, Ford Motor Company, General Motors Corporation
- Becker, Kevin, "Time Accelerated Ultrasonic Testing for Disk Drive Suspension Assemblies", 2005 RAMS Proceedings, IEEE
- Bothe, Davis R., Measuring Process Capability – Techniques and Calculations for Quality and Manufacturing Engineers, 1997, McGraw-Hill Companies, Inc., ISBN 0-07-006652-3
- Deming, W. Edwards, Out of the Crisis, 1986, the W. Edwards Deming Institute
- Devore, Jay L., Probability and Statistics for Engineering and the Sciences 2nd Ed., 1987, Brooks/Cole Publishing Company, ISBN 0-534-06828-6.
- Devore, Jay L. and Peck, Roxy, Statistics: The Exploration and Analysis of Data, 1986, West Publishing Company, ISBN 0-314-93172-4
- Duncan, Acheson J., Quality Control and Industrial Statistics 5th Ed., 1986, Richard D. Irwin, Inc., ISBN 0-256-03535-0
- Ireson, W. Grant, et. al., Handbook of Reliability Engineering and Management 2nd Ed., 1996, McGraw-Hill Companies, Inc., ISBN 0-07-012750-6
- Juran, Joseph M., Godfrey, A. Blanton, Juran's Quality Handbook, 5th Ed., 1999, McGraw-Hill Companies, Inc., ISBN 0-07-034003-X
- Life Data Analysis Reference, ReliaSoft Corporation, 1996, chapter 6
- Modarres, Mohammad, et al, Reliability Engineering and Risk Analysis, A Practical Guide, 1999, Marcel Dekker, Inc.
- Nachtsheim, Christopher J., Becker, Kevin E., "When is R^2 Appropriate for Comparing Customer and Supplier Measurement Systems?", Quality and Reliability Engineering International, 2011, John Wiley and Sons, Ltd.

- Nelson, Wayne B., <u>Accelerated Testing: Statistical Models, Test Plans, and Data Analysis</u>, 2004, John Wiley and Sons, Inc., ISBN 0-471-69736-2
- O'Connor, Patrick D.T., <u>Practical Reliability Engineering 3rd Ed. Revised</u>, 1995, John Wiley and Sons Ltd., ISBN 0-471-96025-X
- Squeglia, Nicholas L., <u>Zero Acceptance Number Sampling Plans, 5th Ed.</u>, 2008, American Society for Quality, ISBN 978-0-87389-739-6

Explanation of selected references:

[Devore, 1987] is the statistics book I first learned with and, as such, the one with which I am most familiar. The book is calculus-based and rather mathematically intense.

[Devore and Peck] is an algebra-based statistics text and as such less mathematically intensive than many of the other listed references.

[Duncan] contains considerable information not present in other texts and explains statistical concepts/methods in greater detail. I find this one particularly useful when trying to understand a given topic in greater depth. It is not shy with the math, including calculus, but supplements this with considerable qualitative information regarding the covered topics.

[Ireson] is a broad overview of reliability engineering principles and methods. While it includes some calculus, much of the information is qualitative and the text is not overly mathematical.

[Modarres] is a general reference for reliability engineering and risk analysis.

[Juran] is widely recognized across the Quality profession. The book covers a wide range of topics. I'm partial to the 5th edition as the 6th is missing many of the useful tables present in the 5th edition.

[Nelson] is widely recognized in Reliability Engineering circles for accelerated testing. The text is rather mathematically intensive.

[O'Connor] is a good introductory reference for Reliability Engineers. Almost all reliability texts include some calculus and this one is no exception. That stated, the text contains considerable qualitative information and is not viewed as overly mathematically intensive.

ASQ/Quality Press is a good source for other reference materials in the fields of Quality and Reliability.

Chapter Synopsis

The synopsis lists intended audience, any background knowledge assumed, and a short description of the material in the chapter.

Chapter 1 – These Parts Need to Ship Today

Intended audience: Quality and Operations department and senior level management, all Quality department personnel.

Description: How to create a culture that promotes superior product, completed on time.

Chapter 2 – Principle-Based Business

Intended audience: General management, all Quality department personnel.

Description: Understand the value of running a principle-based business and the risks/costs with failing to do so. Introduces the concept of **Normalization of Deviance**. Illustrates how having a set of principles as a foundation facilitates decision-making.

Chapter 3 – "In God we trust. . ."

Intended audience: Anyone in a decision-making capacity in business.

Description: Illustrates the importance of making decisions based on data – in combination with proper use of insight or intuition.

Chapter 4 – Maintaining Credibility

Intended audience: Quality department personnel who have to regularly report information related to scrap rates, customer complaints, inadequate CAPA responses, etc.

Description: How to maintain credibility and respect while delivering what is often viewed as "bad" news.

Chapter 5 – Worst Possible Answer

Intended audience: Personnel in a decision-making capacity.

Description: Describes how the worst answers are not only wrong, but also believable.

Chapter 6 – Most Important Part of a QMS . . .

Intended audience: Executive and middle management, Quality department personnel.

Description: Illustrates the importance of management support for any successful quality system.

Chapter 7 – Myth: "We know we've shipped . . ."

Intended audience: Management, Quality, Engineering, and Operations personnel.

Description: Describes the potential pitfalls associated with this particular myth.

Chapter 8 – Myth: As Long As . . .

Intended audience: Quality, Manufacturing, and Design Engineers. General management.

Description: Illustrates how even parts meeting tolerance can cause problems for a customer under certain circumstances.

Chapter 9 – Myth: Quality Is A Given . . .

Intended audience: Executive and middle management.

Description: While rooted in good intentions, this myth can cause practical difficulties as explained in this chapter.

Chapter 10 – Myth: 'Quality Is Free' . . .

Intended audience: General management.

Description: Good return on investment is not the same as no investment required.

Chapter 11 – Myth: The Job of a Quality Inspector/Auditor . . .

Intended audience: General management; Quality, Operations, and Engineering department personnel.

Description: The job is to find and report the truth. It's that simple and that important.

Chapter 12 – Myth: Purchase Price Equals Cost

Intended audience: Buyers, planners, Procurement Engineers, and others in the Purchasing organization in addition to the general audience described at the beginning of this synopsis.

Description: Explains the fallacy that price equals cost and illustrate how saving pennies on purchase price can cost many thousands of dollars, or more, due to losses elsewhere throughout the business.

Chapter 13 – The Importance of Why

Intended audience: Engineers and managers, including senior management, when implementing decisions where the reasons behind those decisions are not obvious to others.

Description: Improve acceptance of the decision and thereby improve cooperation. Explain the risks associated with failure to explain the reasons.

Chapter 14 – Incenting Counterproductive Behaviors

Intended audience: Management, all levels.

Description: Explain how metrics and incentives can have the unintended consequence of promoting behavior opposite to that which is intended. Offer suggestions to avoid this problem.

Chapter 15 – QE Relationship to Auditors and Inspectors

Intended audience: Quality and Reliability engineers, managers, and other department personnel.

Description: Illustrate how Quality and Reliability engineers can avoid ambiguous criteria and make the job easier for almost everyone else.

Chapter 16 – How QE/RE Add Value to a Company

Intended audience: Quality and Reliability Engineers and management.

Description: Provides a comparison of some of the tools available to QE/RE, in particular FTA and FMEA.

Chapter 17 – Rewarding Firefighting

Intended audience: Management, all levels.

Description: Illustrate the costs related to a culture that promotes firefighting and offer suggestions to create a culture of preventing problems instead.

Chapter 18 – Benefits of Regulations and Industry Standards

Intended audience: Management, all levels. Quality and Reliability Engineers.

Description: Illustrate how to use regulations and industry standards to improve, rather than hinder, a business.

Chapter 19 – Internal Competition

Intended audience: Management and others involved in setting and tracking performance metrics.

Description: Explains how internal competition, depending on how it is managed, can either help or hinder a business.

Chapter 20 – Managing Rapid Growth

Intended audience: General management.

Description: Good training is important for any successful business. This importance is magnified many times during periods of rapid growth.

Chapter 21 – Which Is More Important . . .

Intended audience: General management.

Description: It does not provide benefit to efficiently do something we shouldn't be doing at all.

Chapter 22 – Important, Urgent, Both, or Neither?

Intended audience: Personnel subject to time constraints, pressure, and frequent interruptions.

Description: The work is never-ending, so why spend time on unimportant activities?

Chapter 23 – Any Process Can Be Flow Charted

Intended audience: Quality and Manufacturing Engineers

Description: Flow charting is a basic, yet powerful tool for improving both effectiveness and efficiency of almost any quality or manufacturing process.

Chapter 24 – Myth: Correlation = Causation

Intended audience: Engineers and others interested in determining cause and effect.

Description: While correlation may be an important clue, by itself it does not prove causation.

Chapter 25 – Myth: MTBF is the best reliability metric. . .

Intended audience: Reliability and Quality Engineers, technical and senior management.

Description: MTBF is the most commonly abused reliability metric. A non-mathematical explanation is provided explaining why this metric is often wrong, when it is appropriate, and what to use in its place.

Chapter 26 – Set your own course. . .

Intended audience: Anyone making product or process-related decisions, including leaders who may be inadvertently encouraging employees in unethical behavior.

Background required: None

Description: Deals with ethical questions that arise, particularly in the Quality field.

Chapter 27 – Use of r². . .

Intended audience: Quality, Manufacturing, and Design Engineers and technical management.

Background required: Moderate knowledge of statistics, GR&R, and measurement correlation.

Description: R-squared, used improperly, results in wrong decisions and wasteful actions. This chapter explains how the indicator is used incorrectly and provides a comparison and reference to other methods.

Chapter 28 – Control Charts for Monitoring . . .

Intended audience: Quality, Manufacturing, and Design Engineers and technical management.

Background required: Moderate knowledge of SPC.

Description: This is an extension of chapter 26. It explains how SPC can be used to assess measurement correlation and to monitor is ongoing. SPC is better understood and less mathematically intensive than the previous chapter.

Chapter 29 – Cpk and Ppk . . .

Intended audience: Quality, Manufacturing, and Design Engineers and technical management.

Background required: Basic understanding of statistics, capability indices, SPC, histograms, and probability plots.

Description: The difference between Cpk and Ppk is a common source of confusion and the cause of poor decisions. This chapter explains the difference and when/why one should be preferred over the other.

Chapter 30 – Myth: Sampling 10% . . .

Intended audience: Quality, and Manufacturing Engineers and technical management.

Background required: Basic understanding of statistics and sampling.

Description: The stated myth is common because the statistical reasoning behind it is counter-intuitive to many people. This chapter explains why the belief is a myth and offers a brief explanation of how to determine the effect of sampling plan choice on outgoing quality.

Chapter 31 – Myth: A 1.0 AQL . . .

Intended audience: Quality and Manufacturing Engineers, technical management.

Background required: Basic understanding of statistics and sampling.

Description: Many people think that the AQL is the defect rate likely to fail a given sampling plan. In truth, it is the opposite.

Chapter 32 – Myth: If $r^2 < 0.8$ . . .

Intended audience: Quality and Manufacturing Engineers, technical management.

Background required: Basic statistics and understanding of chapter 26.

Description: Emphasizes that r-squared has no relationship to stability/control.

Chapter 33 - Myth: If Cpk < 1.0 ...

Intended audience: Quality, Manufacturing, and Design Engineers and technical management.

Background required: Basic statistics and SPC

Description: This chapter illustrates why a Cpk value cannot be used to determine whether a process is stable/controlled.

Chapter 34 – Data Transformation ...

Intended audience: Quality, Manufacturing, and Design Engineers and technical management.

Background required: Moderate statistics and some familiarity with data transformation.

Description: Data transformation is a valuable statistical method that has recently been abused. This chapter illustrates how the method is abused and steps to take to correct the problem.

Chapter 35 – Myth: 95/95 ...

Intended audience: Quality, Design, and Manufacturing Engineers; technical management.

Background required: General knowledge of confidence/reliability or confidence/conformance statements.

Description: People often use the term "reliability" when they are really talking about "conformance".

Chapter 36 – Designing Time Accelerated Tests

Intended audience: Reliability, Design, and Quality Engineers; technical management.

Background required: This is the most math intensive chapter and requires some knowledge of calculus to fully understand the principles. However, an example is included to implement the method in Minitab without working through the detailed math.

Description: This chapter is based on a technique I developed in the early 2000s while working in the disk drive industry. The original paper was presented at an international reliability conference, 2005 RAMS (Reliability and Maintainability Symposium). The method can be used to develop (time) accelerated test plans for product reliability testing.

Chapter 37 – The Great Unsolved Quality Problem of Our Time

Intended audience: Engineers and managers working to improve quality by preventing, rather than reacting to, problems. Note: the problem is explained, not solved, in this chapter (hence the chapter title). I'd greatly appreciate if you share with me any solution you have developed.

Background required: No special background is required, although the discussion will be more meaningful to someone who has had to justify preventive actions to management.

Description: How do we allocate scarce resources to preventive activities when we can't confidently estimate ROI?

Chapter 38: Derivation for Attribute Sample Size Rule of Thumb

Intended audience: Quality and Manufacturing Engineers; technical management.

Background required: Algebra and basic probability/statistics

Description: One of my college instructors mentioned a simple rule of thumb for calculating required sample size. Every rule of thumb is an approximation and is reasonably accurate over a limited range. This chapter derives the rule of thumb and uses that insight to determine over what range it provides reasonable accuracy or, conversely, when it falls apart.

Chapter 39: Effect of Measurement Error on Process Capability

Intended audience: Quality, Manufacturing, and Design Engineers; technical management.

Background required: Statistics, knowledge of MSA (Measurement System Analysis).

Description: A common criteria for measurement error is acceptable if less than 20% of the tolerance range; acceptable if less than 30% of tolerance with approval. At first glance, this seems excessive. 30% of tolerance is almost 1/3. How can we let measurement error consume this much of the tolerance? When one analyzes the impact to process capability, however, the criteria seem more reasonable. Since standard deviations combine in a RSS (Root Sum of Squares) fashion, the impact to overall capability is less than first imagined.

Chapter 40: Short Bites

Intended audience: A wide range of engineering, management, and quality personnel.

Background required: No special background for much of the chapter. Some algebra and statistics.

Description: This chapter was intended as a compilation of short topics that didn't warrant their own chapter. As it turns out, some of the topics are longer than full chapters in the first edition of this book. Despite this, I opted not to rearrange the chapters from the first edition to incorporate the shorter ones into this chapter. Some topics are intended as instructional, others simply to provide insight into the life of a QE/Quality Manager. Hopefully a few provide amusement.

Chapter 41: Acceptance Sampling for a Highly Capable Process

Intended audience: Quality Engineers and Managers

Background required: Algebra and statistics

Description: Traditional acceptance sampling compares product to tolerance. When we have a highly capable process, the sample size can be reduced dramatically with the same or better level of assurance – as long as we compare against properly derived action limits rather than tolerance limits.